HOWARD FARRAN

UNCOMPLICATE

BUSINESS

ALL IT TAKES IS PEOPLE, TIME, AND MONEY

GREENLEAF
BOOK GROUP PRESS

This publication is designed to provide accurate and authoritative information in regard to the subject matter covered. It is sold with the understanding that the publisher and author are not engaged in rendering legal, accounting, or other professional services. If legal advice or other expert assistance is required, the services of a competent professional should be sought.

Published by Greenleaf Book Group Press
Austin, Texas
www.gbgpress.com

Distributed by Greenleaf Book Group

For ordering information or special discounts for bulk purchases, please contact Greenleaf Book Group at PO Box 91869, Austin, TX 78709, 512.891.6100.

Design and composition by Greenleaf Book Group
Cover design by Greenleaf Book Group

The Paradoxical Commandments reprinted with the permission of the author. © Kent M. Keith 1968, renewed 2001.
Cartoon (ID: med15), reprinted by permission of the artist/author, © Randy Glasbergen.
Excerpts from *The Psychology of Waiting Lines*, by David Maister, reprinted by permission from the author (http://davidmaister.com/articles/the-psychology-of-waiting-lines/).
© 1985 by David Maister.
Email message reprinted by permission of the author, Garrett Gunderson.

Cataloging-in-Publication data is available.

ISBN: 978-1-62634-179-1

Part of the Tree Neutral® program, which offsets the number of trees consumed in the production and printing of this book by taking proactive steps, such as planting trees in direct proportion to the number of trees used: www.treeneutral.com

TreeNeutral®

Printed in the United States of America on acid-free paper

15 16 17 18 19 20   10 9 8 7 6 5 4 3 2 1

First Edition

Other Edition(s)
eBook ISBN: 978-1-62634-180-7

I'm dedicating this book to the perfect yin to my yang: Lorie Xelowski. Since 1998 we have been bound by a common devotion to hard work, professional challenges, and the love of business.

I am a gregarious extrovert. I love to share my ideas loudly and with as many people as possible. Lorie is a quiet introvert, like Eleanor Roosevelt or Gandhi, and she has been the best business partner a guy like me could have ever hoped for. I may express my ideas loudly and move on to the next topic without blinking, but Lorie has always been able to take these grandiose ideas, delete more than half of them, give shape to the ones she thinks have a chance, and then make them happen.

I would not be as successful as I am today without Lorie. I am deeply indebted to her and thankful that we continue working together to this very day.

In looking for a partner, you need to find someone with massive integrity, dedication to hard work, and intellectual curiosity—qualities that, in my book, make her a genius.

Acknowledgments

I would like to express my gratitude to the many people who saw me through this book: to all those who provided support, talked things over, read, wrote, offered comments, or assisted in the editing, proofreading, and design. This book has come to fruition because of the community around me.

I would like to personally thank a few people who went above and beyond.

First of all, Lorie Xelowski. Lorie has been my right-hand woman for fifteen years. Her title is president of my media company, but, ultimately, she does all the operational logistics. She facilitates my crazy ideas and helps me execute them in the company and the practice. This book is dedicated to her.

Thanks to Ben Lund, who, as editor of my media company from 2006 to 2013, helped me build seven years of "Howard Speaks" columns. Much of the information in this book is taken from these columns.

Thanks to Charlotte Brown, my editor, who took this book from rough draft to developmental edit to line edit. She tamed my brash expressions, but kept my voice and message intact. Her patience and expertise are so appreciated.

Thanks to Tim Lott, friend and CPA, who contributed to the money section of this book. He gave me average numbers for the financials/cash flow statements.

Thanks to Sandy Wilkinson, Valerie Williams, and Jan Sweeney. They are the intellect and fortitude behind what makes my dental practice run smoothly.

Marcie Donavon and Stacie Holub, both managers at the media company (and the three women mentioned previously) all contributed to sidebars within the book. Their added information enriches the content.

This book was a collective effort. I am grateful to the many who were involved in this process.

CONTENTS

SECTION II: TIME

Introduction

"So how does a dentist make so much money?"

That's what my dad, by then a successful entrepreneur himself, asked as he and I pulled into our driveway and saw our neighbor chipping golf balls into a Hula-Hoop, just as we had seen him do many times before. As we waved to our neighbor Kenny Anderson, a local dentist, Dad turned to me and said, "Howie, if you had half a brain in your head you'd become a dentist."

Growing up in Wichita, Kansas, I was one of seven kids. My mother stayed at home while my father spent his days scratching out a meager living as a bread deliveryman. Dad toiled more than twelve hours a day, seven days a week, yet the Farran family had a hard time paying the bills. On Sundays, we'd take two cars to church where Dad would sit with us for eight o'clock Mass before driving on to the Rainbow Bread Company to start his shift delivering bread to grocery stores. For the first ten years of my life, if I ever wanted to see my dad, I had to ride with him on his delivery route.

One day my father came home excited to tell us about a friend and coworker who saved up a bunch of cash, took out a loan, left his job delivering bread, and purchased a Sonic Drive-In fast-food franchise. In just months it was making a killing and the guy was raking in more cash in a month than he'd see in a year driving a truck. His story got Dad's gears spinning. For days it was all he could talk about. I'd never seen my father so revved up about anything. He saw it as a great opportunity to do something about his insufficient income and provide better lives for us.

In the ensuing weeks, during whatever time away from work he could muster, my father spent with his friend, either on the phone or at his drive-in. He knew he could do as good a job as his friend and decided taking on a franchise was worth the risk.

Can you imagine how much courage it took for a guy supporting a wife and seven kids—a bread deliveryman with little business acumen—to bet everything he had on a fast-food franchise? Sure, if it didn't work out, he could go back to delivering bread, but he was driven to make it work. Outwardly my father was the king of cool about it; he might have been stressed out of his mind making this decision, but if he was, we never knew it.

Hindsight being 20/20, buying his first Sonic franchise was the best decision my father ever made. Over the next ten years, our family went from abject poverty to becoming fairly wealthy, as my dad accumulated nine Sonic restaurants in four states. My relationship with my father didn't change much. While my friends threw the ball around in the back yard or went camping with their dads, spending time with my dad still meant tagging along with him at work. But man, when I went to work with my dad, I was the proudest little boy in the world. I got to watch my dad run his business . . . and he was good at it! Handling customers, managing his employees, watching overhead, placing orders, stepping in where help was needed—my father made it all look effortless.

Through my father's risks and eventual success, I witnessed first-hand the power of self-employment, business, marketing, advertising, and human relations. I learned early on the three keys to business: how to make something, how to sell it, and how to watch the numbers to ensure you stay in business. And I started to make observations that led to the idea behind this book—that the uncomplicated heart of business success lies in the ability to manage three things: people, time, and money. Dad nurtured in me a personality hardwired for business.

I took my dad's advice and set my sights on becoming a dentist like our neighbor with the ever more expert chip shot. As a teenager—when I wasn't at school or at my job flipping burgers for Dad at his Sonic drive-in—I took it upon myself to visit some local dental practices just to see if it was something I'd really like. Long story short—I was hooked.

A dentist started the day at eight o'clock in the morning and closed the office at five in the afternoon. Dad's drive-in opened at the same hour, but didn't close for the day until eleven thirty at night Sunday through Thursday, and not until well after midnight on Fridays and Saturdays. The dentist performed intellectually challenging work and never went home with soggy, wrinkled feet from hosing down floors and sidewalks. And absent of the continuous drama among the post-pubescent restaurant staff, the dentist's office felt downright serene.

When I was seventeen, my father sat me down and told me that there are two kinds of people: those who look for free fish and those who get a fishing pole. He assured me there were no free fish to be found in the Farran household, so if I wanted to make something of myself (and I did!), I'd have to find a pole and catch some fish.

From that point on, I was on my own. I put myself through college, doing my undergrad at Creighton University in three years. I then put myself through dental school at the University of Missouri–Kansas City.

Like my dad, my mother held strong opinions regarding what made for a fulfilling and comfortable life. Whenever she watched the weather reports on television, she noticed that the Mr. Sunshine icon always hovered over Phoenix, Arizona.

"Howie," she once said to me, "If you had half a brain in your head, you'd move to Phoenix where the sun shines all the time."

So on September 21, 1987—just four months after graduation—I took Mom's advice and opened my own dental practice in Phoenix.

Howard as a child

(TOP Left to right): Gene Farran, Jeanmarie Murry (Howard's sister), Colleen Farran (Howard's Mother), (BOTTOM Left to right) Kellie Schmitz (Howard's sister), Kaleen Farran (Howard's sister), Shelly Jones, Sr. Anne of Yahweh Farran (Howard's sister), and Howard Farran

Howard's father's message to him at graduation (he owned the Sonic Drive-In)

(Left to right): Gene Farran (Howard's father), Howard Farran, Kellie Farran (Howard's sister), Mother Mary Magdene O'Halloran (as a child), and Shelly Jones (Howard's sister)

Howard Farran and Paul Farran (Howard's brother)

Howard Farran and Michael DiTolla, DDS, 1994, breaking ground on the new Today's Dental Building

I had reached my goal. I was a dentist with my own practice at the age of twenty-four. I also had a wife, $87,000 in student loans, a home mortgage of $98,000, and a $150,000 business loan.

I was scared to death! How was I going to get back to zero, let alone get ahead? Fortunately, I am my father's kid. Dad used to say, "Remember, work like no man has for a decade and you can reap like no man has for the rest of your life."

I took that to heart. I busted my butt, twelve hours a day, six days a week. (Unlike Dad, I gave myself most Sundays off.) I went door to door and met everybody in my neighborhood—as though I were running for mayor. Any patient who wanted to see me, Monday through Saturday, could get in. I made room. I'd even come in on Sundays for emergencies. Before long, I was debt free. It may be clichéd, but, in my experience, there is no easier, better way to pay off any debt than good old-fashioned hard work.

Once my loans were paid off, I turned all of my attention to my practice. Most of my business knowledge I learned from my father— but most of his business knowledge came purely from instinct. I didn't know if my practice was operating properly. Every day, I'd wonder how much of what my father taught me was educationally sound.

Dental schools teach clinical skills such as how to fill cavities. They do not teach dentists how to hire employees, fill vacancies in their schedule, or cut overhead. Even if business classes were offered as an elective, dental students probably wouldn't see the value in taking them. Like lawyers, priests, accountants, engineers, and other professionals, they focus on their product rather than on the bottom line. (I have a friend, a Catholic priest who, after eight years in the seminary, discovered he still knew nothing about running a church or an elementary school.)

In 1999, I got fed up with my—and my colleagues'—lack of business acumen and decided to take matters into my own hands. In addition to getting more training in implantology, endodontics, and other dental specialties, I got a master of business administration from Arizona State University. In just a few years, I turned myself from an everyday small businessman into a successful entrepreneur.

Howard Farran lecturing

Howard Farran and his father, Gene Farran

Today I own a booming practice along with a multimillion-dollar dental media company and seminar business designed to connect dentists from all over the world and share practical information to help keep their businesses profitable.

Dentists are businesspeople. Sure, I spend a lot of time poking around in people's mouths. But step back from the clinical aspects, and a dental practice is really no different than any small business. The same simple fundamentals remain. Like anyone in business, dentists have to produce a product, sell the product, and generate a profit. They have to manage their people, their time, and their money. They have to deliver excellent customer service and achieve balance between personal life and work. And most of them don't make as much money as they should. Sound familiar?

I likely would have chosen a different career had my father known that many dentists are lousy businesspeople who struggle to make a living. That's among the reasons some dentists get involved with substance abuse and have one of the highest suicide rates of any profession.

After revolutionizing my practice, I started a dental magazine and an online community to help my colleagues improve their practices as well. The website is now the largest online dental community—an interactive healthcare community working to connect dentists to their peers, dental service providers, and manufacturers. The dental magazine currently is mailed to dentists across the U.S. and in forty-three countries each month, and sent digitally to every country on earth. On our flagship website, dental professionals share information with each other on a daily basis. Two additional publications and websites for orthodontists and hygienists serve professionals throughout the dental industry, even offering more than two hundred continuing education courses on topics ranging from fixed prosthodontics and digital radiography, to personal finance and marketing.

In addition, my company runs an annual "Townie Meeting" convention for all dental professionals interested in education, entertainment, and camaraderie. Nothing like helping out the competition, is there? Then again, I firmly believe that a rising tide lifts all boats.

That takes me back to why I wrote this book. I want to help lift your boat to the highest level of success by helping you see that business success need not be complicated or intimidating.

This book is for you if:

- you are wondering whether you have what it takes to start and achieve a successful business,
- you already have a business but are struggling to keep it afloat,

- you want to turn your modestly successful business into a megahit, and
- you want to achieve your goal in the *simplest, fastest, and most time-tested ways.*

In my consulting work, I have helped thousands of dentists correct almost every kind of basic business mistake—mistakes common to all businesses—and watched them turn their struggles into successes.

Even if you don't have an MBA (although I highly recommend getting one), learning a few key concepts will help you build a successful business. This book is designed to demystify and simplify those core concepts for you, whether you're just starting to think about self-employment or have run a business for years and need a refresh. We won't be diving into complex theoretical discussions—just the straightforward practices that will improve your operation and maximize your success, whether you sell comic books, run a chain of fast-food restaurants, or are the CEO of a Fortune 500 company.

I've organized these concepts into three categories that form the structure of the following chapters:

People. You have to know how to get the most out of people: your employees, your colleagues, your customers, and yourself.

Time. Efficiency is the name of the game here. The more efficiently you run your business, the more money you will make. Technology is the key to turning time into money.

Money. Money is the scorecard for how well your business is doing. Without sufficient cash flow, you can't reinvest in your business at the level that enables it to grow. If you want to do what you love to do, you need to learn to love watching the numbers.

People, time, and money—those three are all it takes. If you're able to manage each of them well, you're going to have a financially healthy business and a fulfilling life as an entrepreneur. As we explore how to do that, you'll be hearing not just from me but also from some of my employees—exemplary people who share my passion for the work that we do and who have a lot to say about the fundamentals of a successful business.

I know you're busy, so let's get started. Sit back in your chair, relax, and in a few minutes you'll be feeling a whole lot better about your business.

If you can dream it, you can achieve it.

—*Zig Ziglar*

SECTION 1

PEOPLE

Introduction

I once had a neighbor in the rubber gasket business. He made rubber gaskets that connect and seal two metal pieces to prevent fluids from leaking. He was passionate about his product, about making the best gaskets on the planet. That may seem an inconsequential endeavor compared to performing a heart transplant or launching a space shuttle. But tell that to the guy who didn't get his new heart in time because his ambulance broke down on the way to the hospital due to a faulty gasket in the engine. Or to the families of the crew on the Space Shuttle Columbia disaster who lost their loved ones due to a faulty O-ring—a gasket. My neighbor is a multimillionaire because of his passion for building the best gaskets he can.

He could trace his passion back to his childhood. He and I grew up in the same era, when you had to learn how to fix your own car—replace broken water hoses, patch tires and change gaskets—if you wanted it to be running on time for your date Friday night.

My friend became passionate about fixing engines, which grew into a passion for improving on the quality of the parts. That eventually led to his business, which made him a millionaire. And all because he knew who he was, what he felt passionate about, and what he wanted to achieve.

Who are you? What are you passionate about? What do you want to achieve?

The first element of uncomplicated business is people. Every business is designed by people, run by people, and made to serve people, so it's no surprise that this is where we begin our journey. In the following chapters, we'll look at you (you're a person, after all) as well as the people you employ and the people your business serves.

1

Know Yourself

The most important person in your business is you. Your business is an extension of you—an extension of your personality and character. Until you know who you are and what you bring to your business, you can't begin to understand your employees, your customers, your vendors—anyone.

When it comes to business, the most important question to ask yourself is: *Am I really cut out to run a business?*

Sure, it may feel good to brag to the gang at the gym that you own and run your own business. It feels even better if you are able to say you own and run a successful business. Yet not everyone has what it takes to run a successful business. As you work with other people, you need to be aware of your personal strengths and weaknesses. Some of who you are depends on your genes, but a lot of your personality depends on where you grew up. If you are going to be a successful businessperson, you have to understand the roots of your personality.

As I said, I have the personality of a successful businessperson. I was hardwired for success from childhood. I witnessed my father's successes firsthand. From his and my mother's examples—for better or for worse—I learned three valuable lessons.

From the strength and depth of their religious beliefs, I learned that there is a purpose and power to life that not only extends well beyond me, but also resides within me.

From the exclusionary nature of their beliefs, I learned about the separation created when love and acceptance are conditional upon sharing those beliefs. So I chose the path of acceptance and unconditional love instead.

From seeing my father exploited by business partners and landlords, I learned the value of self-reliance. To borrow from the old American proverb, I learned to love many, trust few, and paddle my own canoe.

These childhood lessons serve not only as the foundation of my personal life but also my professional life.

I share all of this to make the point that making the effort to examine and understand where you came from—what shaped you—will help provide a firm foundation upon which to build your business.

It also helps to examine the business role models you had growing up.

George Steinbrenner was one of my heroes. If you don't know his story, he was the owner of the New York Yankees, who passed away from a heart attack on July 13, 2010, at the age of eighty. "The Boss" was one of the most polarizing people in professional baseball; he was lauded as much as he was criticized. He operated the most scrutinized professional sports team in America's most scrutinizing market—New York—but he had very thick skin and was true to himself. And it paid off; over the course of the thirty-seven years he owned the Yankees, his team won seven World Series titles and eleven pennants. The value of the team went from $8.8 million to $1.5 billion.

No matter where you came from, what sort of upbringing you had, you can develop the kind of personality you need to run a successful business.

How do you do that? Train yourself to have good business habits.

If you make it a personal habit to brush and floss your teeth every morning when you wake up and every night before you go to bed, you're not going to be one of the 25 percent of sixty-five-year-old and older Americans who have no teeth in their mouths. If you make it a personal habit to exercise forty minutes a day, then it's more likely that you'll live a longer life and you'll feel better about yourself. These are small things that you apply to your daily life, but they all add up in the big scheme of things.

The same is true of your business personality. If you want to change the biggest things about your business, you must work on the smallest things. You need to understand who you are and be willing to develop the good, positive ways of thinking that will enable you to run a successful business. You're the business owner—you're the spine and central nervous system of this company, so what traits do you bring to the table in order to direct your company to success?

It helps if you have a decent balance of left-brain (analytical) and right-brain (creative) thinking, but we all lean more toward one or the other. I'm very much a left-brain, critical thinker; I thrive on analytical information that can give me specific measurements on which I can base success. Whichever way you lean, it helps to bolster the "weaker" side of your brain among your employee base. As I wrote in my dedication, and will expand on later, Lorie, the president of my media company, is the perfect balance for my strengths and weaknesses.

Know the weaknesses as well as the strengths you bring to your business. I assert it is more important to know your weaknesses than your strengths—to honestly examine what skills you lack that other people can provide to help you succeed.

In any line of work, there are things we know we love to do and do well. Dentists love doing dentistry—that's what we went to school from eight to twelve years for—but for the most part, we aren't all that good at running our own businesses. That's why I, and many others, have office managers to assist in the day-to-day operations of our practices.

Finally, don't let anyone make you doubt yourself or your passion. When faced with critics, remember the words of Theodore Roosevelt:

Far better it is to dare mighty things, to win glorious triumphs even though checkered by failure, than to rank with those timid spirits who neither enjoy nor suffer much because they live in the gray twilight that knows neither victory nor defeat.

ACTION POINTS

- Know your background.
    - List the three most important lessons you learned from your parents.
    - Identify business role models you had, either in person or through books, while you were growing up.
- Know your personality.
    - List the five personality traits that make you successful.
    - List the strengths you bring to a business.
    - Honestly examine your weaknesses. List the skills you lack that other people will need to provide to help you succeed.

He who knows others is wise;
he who knows himself is enlightened.

—Lao Tzu

2

Leadership

Once you examine your background, habits, strengths, and weaknesses, you need to ask yourself, "Do I know what it takes to be a leader?"

Your business is *your business*. You are the one who is going to benefit the most from running it. Whether you make it successful will depend on much more than the education and training you got in school.

I find it funny how impressed many people are with the skill set of a cardiovascular surgeon or a dentist doing a root canal. In performing a coronary artery bypass graft, a cardiovascular surgeon is repeating a skill she trained for in medical school: replacing a pipe in a heart that's clogged up with nasty fat. She cuts it out, finds a cleaner pipe in the patient's leg, cuts out a chunk of that pipe and puts it in the heart in place of the clogged one. Voila! It sounds impressive, but in reality it's a learned skill that almost any reasonably well-coordinated individual could perform. Just as, after adequate training, a cardiovascular surgeon could manage to replumb a house.

And a root canal? C'mon! You drill a hole in the middle of a tooth. You take the artery, vein, and nerve out; clean it out; and fill it with cement. The people I really respect are psychiatrists and psychologists. In this day and age, these professionals are the equivalent to Galileo at a time when everybody thought the earth was flat. They aren't just performing technical operations; they are discovering how the brain works, something we're not going to be able to completely understand for centuries, if at all. To run a successful business, you need to know how to lead people to work for you, work with you, and patronize your business.

As an avid reader, I've read hundreds of books on business—books that suggest to me that, as a CEO, I must be a magician, motivator, leader, charismatic, tall, dark, handsome, and capable of riding a unicycle while juggling bowling pins, just to get everyone to follow me.

I disagree. Leadership is much simpler. To be a leader, you've simply got to be a winner.

George Steinbrenner once said: "Winning is the most important thing in my life, after breathing. Breathing first, winning next."

Steinbrenner was always the first to admit he didn't make all the right decisions (after all, he did hire and fire manager Billy Martin five times), but he was the most successful owner of the winningest professional sports club in North America. He is an excellent example of what leadership is all about.

Steinbrenner knew that he needed to lead five categories of people to build a winning team: fans, players, managers, other team owners, and himself. From studying hundreds of CEOs, I discovered the winning characteristics necessary for me to be a good leader in my business.

CHARACTERISTICS OF A LEADER

A leader is humble. A lot of people have trouble with this one and I get that. A dentist comes out of eight years of dental school ready to champion the oral health of an entire town, and such an achievement comes with a little bluster. But the credentials that go with any highly trained professional don't give that person the right to be a highfalutin jerk. You can't look down your nose at anyone—certainly not your employees or your customers. You have to be a leader.

I've had mothers of young patients come in and say, "If I don't give my baby Mountain Dew, she'll cry."

Rather than chew the woman out for not knowing the connection between sugar and tooth decay, I remain calm and respectful. I exist to be of service, not to criticize. So I say, "Okay, but what is your baby doing right now? She's crying. She's crying because she has a toothache, and it could be caused by the Mountain Dew. You only did what you thought was right, but it's my job to tell you what you need to know so that your daughter keeps her teeth for the rest of her life."

A leader embraces and drives innovation. You have to adopt all technology that helps you do your job faster, easier, at higher quality and lower cost. Macroeconomics is made up of three things: people, technology, and capital. Embrace all new technology. If you study Wall Street from 1792 to 2000, technology is what has driven the market, from steam engines to ship building, railroads to canal building, the telegraph, telephone, automobile, assembly line, radio, television, and the biggest technology boom in my lifetime—the Internet. I always tell young people in high school and college that, by the time they're my age, there's a good chance they'll be working in an industry that hasn't even been invented yet. The biggest millionaires and billionaires of all time are the ones who jumped on a brand new technology. Today it's apps on the Internet, natural gas fracking . . . There's always something new. Learn everything about the new technology in your industry, because likely that will give you a huge competitive advantage.

A leader follows the golden rule: "Treat others just as you would want to be treated." The Golden Rule is first found in Hinduism and then in every major religion thereafter. I love its simplicity. As a business owner and professional in the dental field, I want the trust of my employees. And if I want them to trust me, I had better be willing to trust them, or my business will suffer. The same holds true for any business. If you can't learn how to delegate duties to the right people, you will never be successful.

When someone calls up your business and your employees don't have your permission and trust to answer the person's questions, there's something wrong. Ray Kroc, founder of McDonald's, knew he couldn't make McDonald's a massive franchise if he insisted on doing everything himself. Consequently, today more than 33,000 McDonald's franchises serve up burgers and fries every single day all over the world.

I've never met a millionaire who hasn't mastered delegation. You have to learn to let go. You can't be a control freak.

A leader knows mistakes will be made, is accepting and/or accountable, and moves forward. You're not perfect. Nobody is. There's a reason why, in dentistry, we call it a "dental practice"; nobody has perfected it, and nobody ever will. We are our own worst critics. If someone screws up, help them realize their mistake, redirect if needed, and then move forward. Don't laugh, chastise, or belittle them. Mistakes are an opportunity to learn. In the words of the late author and motivational speaker, Zig Ziglar, "If you learn from defeat, you haven't really lost."

Which brings me to my next point:

A leader never stops learning! No matter how much education or training you have, you don't know everything. The minute you think you do, you're in trouble. If you want to run a successful business, you must keep learning for the rest of your life. You will have to develop a hunger for new knowledge and the mental agility to continuously adapt your business to changing circumstances. Like an athlete who must exercise to stay in shape, you've got to exercise your brain, your "thought muscle." Expose yourself to new ideas as often as you can.

I've worked with a lot of dentists who get out of dental school, become an associate dentist for a dental practice and spend all of their time filling cavities. Learning how to fill a cavity in dental school is pretty intense, but once you're out in the real world, it gets boring. Doing strictly bread-and-butter dentistry, outsourcing procedures like root canals, dental implant placement, and simple orthodontics, has lead many practicing dentists to burn out. There are so many other specialties dentists can learn to apply to their practices in order to do more for their patients.

For years, I have nudged dentists to branch out, expand their thinking, and learn how to do something new. About seven years ago, I had a discussion with a dear friend of mine, Dr. Jay Reznick, a board-certified oral and maxillofacial surgeon—considered by most as one of the best in the business. He practices in Tarzana, California—a suburb of Los Angeles—where there are almost more oral surgeons than there are Starbucks. Jay assumed that most general dentists had an oral surgeon down the street to whom they could send their patients whenever they needed treatment. He did not realize that the majority of dentists in this country, and in fact the world, practice in small communities where there is not the same degree of specialist support as there is in his own town. He also did not realize that a majority of community dentists with family-oriented practices were faced almost daily with patients who needed basic oral surgery care, yet felt uncomfortable treating these patients because of the very limited oral surgery training they received in dental school. Many times, referral of the patient to the oral surgeon was impractical, either due to distance or to the amount of time the patient had to wait for an appointment.

I told Jay there was a real need for quality continuing education in oral surgery for the general practitioner, so that these dentists would feel more confident in their knowledge and competency in surgical skills. Knowing how difficult it was for many dentists to take time away from their practices and travel to continuing education courses, I suggested that he think about producing some educational DVDs to help those general dentists who perform oral surgery procedures in their practices become better clinicians.

Jay spent about a year looking at the oral surgery courses that were already available on DVD, outlining a basic curriculum and looking at new technologies to allow him to show the viewer exactly what he wanted. After all this planning, Jay realized a series of DVD courses was insufficient. He took the concept to the next level by developing a website: www.onlineoralsurgery.com. Jay set up a permanent three-camera video studio in one of his surgical suites so that procedures could be recorded as they happened each day in his busy practice. He then worked day and night editing video and putting together the first video courses. Jay took this on as his mission to better educate those general dentists who couldn't refer but were afraid to take the leap into oral surgery.

A leader is passionate, enthusiastic, and determined to make a difference. Continuing to expand your thinking and your business is important, for sure, but it's just as necessary to infuse your business with soul, with *passion*. You have to think positively and passionately about your business. Your business is a reflection of you, your mission, what you intend to provide to your customers, and how you intend to provide it. If you don't have a passion for what you do (if you're only in this to make a quick buck), then chances are you're not going to have a team that's able to "sell" what you do for your customers. Just as bad, if you have passion for what you do but cannot convey it to your team in a way that makes them passionate about it, too, you'll never get off the ground.

You need to make it a habit to think about your business, and you've got to let others know what you are thinking.

That's something my neighbor with the thriving gasket company and I have in common. We love to think about our work. We love to share our thoughts with others. Most of all, we *love to work*. I always feel bad for high school students when someone asks them what they want to do when they "grow up." The focus is too centered on vocation. The better question is, "How are you learning to love work?" Because my neighbor and I love to work, I bet (with a little education) that if we switched places—if he ran my dental practice and I ran his gasket company—not much would change. If I truly thought I could improve the gasket business, because I'm passionate about working, I know I could do it.

A leader is honest and respectful. Integrity is everything. You have to report your cash, because if you don't, then your employees think it's okay to steal from the IRS, therefore it's okay to steal from you. You have to warranty all your work. You have to be honest. If you screw up, you tell a customer, "Hey I'm a human, and I just broke the burr off into your nerve, and this is what I'm going to do." Don't cover it up. Don't lie. It just makes things worse. Be honest; get it all out.

A leader balances personal life and work and is fully present in both. If you consistently ignore your family, don't be surprised when your family starts ignoring you.

A leader strives to make everyone feel safe, valued, and important. I love the story of Paul O'Neill, the successful chairman and CEO of the aluminum giant Alcoa—a company whose profits increased from $1.5 billion in 1987 (when O'Neill took the reins) to $23 billion in 2000 (when he retired). When he started, he noticed a lot of dysfunction among his teams. The unions weren't agreeing with management, and sales people weren't getting along with engineers. He thought about what common denominator the entire company could care about in order to move them all in the right direction.

The aluminum industry involves extremely hazardous work. Whenever you're heating aluminum to more than 1,000 degrees, you're putting people in danger. A lot of the factory union people didn't want new, high-tech machinery because even though the new machines would be safer to use, the union guys thought that would mean layoffs. They were trying to protect jobs, yet their stubbornness was getting people killed with old machinery.

After O'Neill took over, whenever someone was injured on the job, he demanded that in less than twenty-four hours, a report be on his desk detailing what went wrong and what steps would be taken to fix the problem.

So what happened? When somebody got injured, there was no time for the type of posturing that typically happened—even when someone died. It was a new policy—a new habit—that the entire company could rally around and support fully. There wasn't a single person in that company—no matter what team they were on—who could sit there and say they didn't care about some kid who got a bucket of liquefied, 1,000-degree aluminum dumped on him. How could anyone even think of arguing against new equipment when confronted with Smitty lying dead on the floor, leaving behind a wife and kids thanks to outdated machinery? Instead the people in the field were saying, "Hey, the boss wants to know right now what went wrong. Smitty died and we need to find a solution so it never ever happens again." Factory baloney, union baloney, management baloney, political baloney—all that took a back seat, because if that report didn't make it to O'Neill's desk in twenty-four hours, there would be hell to pay. O'Neill made darn sure of it, too, because word got around pretty quickly that if you didn't have that report on his desk, O'Neill would be on a helicopter and in your face that same day. Safety was the new habit every single person at Alcoa needed to learn and learn fast. All the chains of command at Alcoa changed. The dysfunction started leaving, everybody came together to work toward making a better company, and Alcoa's profits soared. As injuries went to zero, profitability skyrocketed!

Now, most of us will never be as great a leader as Paul O'Neill, but none of us can hope to manage people unless we become leaders.

A leader is remarkably helpful. Empower your staff. Be helpful. Coach them. Invest in training your team, and when they are finished with training, get them some more! If you want to maximize a return on investment, try keeping your employees for life!

DEVELOP YOUR CORE VALUES

My staff and I feel so strongly about these leadership qualities that we adopted and adhere to them as ten of the twelve core values that drive every facet of my business, which are displayed in the lobby of both my dental practice and media company.

Our Core Values

- Create a fun, positive, and professional environment.
- Be passionate, enthusiastic, and determined to make a difference.
- Be humble.
- Embrace and drive innovation.
- Follow the Golden Rule—"Treat others like you would want to be treated."

- Mistakes will be made; be accepting and/or accountable and move forward.
- Never stop learning.
- Be honest and respectful—integrity is everything.
- Balance life and work and be fully present in both.
- Strive to make everyone feel safe, valued, and important.
- Be remarkably helpful.
- Create opportunities to make our customers feel special.

Our final core value prompts our team to "create opportunities to make our customers feel special." I'll have more to say about that in a later chapter. For now I simply want to stress that, while being clear about your purpose and your core values is important, *following* your own core values is critical. You might spend a year coming up with your company's mission statement and core values, but without consistent follow through, they don't mean a darn thing. When you review your employees, you must hold them accountable to all of your company's values. The staff should also have the freedom to police each other. If someone's behavior isn't in line with any of your core values, that person needs to be called out and held accountable for their actions. Everyone should have the opportunity to change their ways, but bottom line, if someone on the team is consistently failing to adhere to your company's values, perhaps it's time that person find another company whose values are more in line with their own.

ACTION POINTS

- Examine your thinking.
- Critically examine your business attitude toward learning.
- Honestly determine whether or not you can be passionate about your work.

- Consider whether you are lacking in certain leadership qualities and what actions indicate you are lacking in those areas.
- Define five specific actions that you will take to improve your leadership abilities.
- Construct a daily "mental exercise" plan for improving your thinking, e.g. making lists, reading books, listening to audio books or TED Talks (online talks that serve to bring together people from three worlds: Technology, Entertainment, and Design).

A leader is best when people know he exists,
when his work is done, his aim fulfilled,
they will say: we did it ourselves.

—*Lao Tzu*

It is better to lead from behind and to put
others in front, especially when you celebrate
victory when nice things occur. You take the
front line when there is danger. Then people
will appreciate your leadership.

—*Nelson Mandela*

3

Purpose

DEVELOP YOUR PURPOSE

My dental career has always been filled with purpose. Within six months of opening up my dental practice in 1987 in Phoenix, Arizona, I was utterly demoralized. I had come from Kansas City, where the tooth decay rate in children was so much lower than the rate in children in Phoenix. I could not understand what was going on. Every mouth of every child I saw was riddled with rotting cavities. I was so baffled I called the local office of dental health and spoke with a man who turned out to be the smartest dentist I've ever met in my life, Dr. Jack Dillenberg. Jack simply said, "It's because Phoenix's water supply isn't fluoridated." I told him I felt like I'd be wasting forty years on an assembly line, drilling, filling, and billing for no purpose at all. I wasn't going to make a dent in this pile. Jack agreed with me and suggested we start a group called the Arizona Citizens for Better Dental Health and get the Phoenix water supply fluoridated. I couldn't say no. We met every Friday for two years until we convinced the city of Phoenix to add fluoride to its drinking water. I lived all week for that Friday meeting with Jack; it gave me such amazing professional purpose.

During that time, I'd speak at local schools and teach the children the importance of good home dental care with lots of brushing and flossing. My goal was to noticeably improve the overall dental health of my community. It still is. It is my purpose!

No matter what your business, you need a purpose!

McDonald's purpose is to provide its customers with fast, convenient, affordable meals in a friendly and fun place to eat.

The purpose of Nordstrom department stores is "to provide outstanding service every day, one customer at a time." Sometimes you have to beat these people off with a stick to shop alone for five seconds, but they are groomed to be servants to the client.

Disney's core purpose is simple: make people happy. How do they do it? With imagination and attention to detail.

Are you aware of how many people never fully realize their purpose? There are people who have lived their entire lives without figuring it out. Ask any pastor how many times a parishioner has asked how to know what God's purpose is for them.

WRITE YOUR MISSION STATEMENT

You need to give your entire company a purpose. I don't just mean your staff, or you, or the chairs, or the bricks, or the mortar, but the driving philosophy of your *entire company*.

Your company's *purpose* gives you clear-cut direction. If you take a team of people who place a high value on profitability, every decision they make will go toward maximizing profits. On the other hand, you might have a group of people who highly value customer care and will do and spend almost anything to make sure their customers are well taken care of. Put those two groups together and you're going to see some battles. One team might want to hold back on spending money in order to lower overhead, while the other team really wants to implement something new to offer customers at the expense of the bottom line.

A mission statement explains to your customers and your team what

your goal is and why your business exists. A mission stat
make your core values and their purpose crystal clear.

Southwest Airlines' mission statement is: "Southwest Airlines is a company that is for anyone and everyone that wants to get from point A to point B by flying. Our service and philosophy is to fly safe, with high frequency, low-cost flights that can get passengers to their destinations on time and often closer to their destination. We fly in 58 cities and 30 states and are the world's largest short-haul carrier, and we make sure that it is run efficiently and in a economical way." In eighty succinct words Southwest Airlines lays out exactly what it does, and if you've ever flown Southwest, it's apparent that its employees take this mission statement to heart.

The mission statement for my dental practice, Today's Dental, reads, "Build a long-term relationship between our staff and patients, and provide quality consumer-friendly dental services the whole family can value and afford in a happy environment." Now tell me you aren't sure what we do after you read that. When my team and I started Today's Dental, we worked on this mission statement for a long time. When we set out, we never wanted to be a cosmetic-only practice with a spa-like setting. Yes, we do some cosmetic work, but we focus on bread-and-butter dentistry, and we aim to please. No frills, happy staff, solid relationships, and good dentistry. This mission statement is not just what we do day in and day out at the practice; it's what we stand for! We live by this mission statement every single day, and if we feel as though we aren't, we retool to make sure we're getting back to our core mission.

GIVE YOUR STAFF A PURPOSE

Late in the French Revolution, as Napoleon took over his battered nation's army, he came to the realization that his opponents were merely unorganized bands of angry mercenaries—thugs who were simply paid money to fight. Napoleon felt his opponents didn't fight with valor, honor, or purpose, so he developed an elaborate system to motivate his own army and give them a strong purpose for fighting. He handed out badges, medals, and other awards for acts of heroism and valor because his men were taking risks for their country. Napoleon changed his army from a bunch of pay-for-play brutes into an honorable fighting force. He spoke at length about fighting with a purpose and his army *dominated*. His army consisted of men who were willing and wanted to fight and, if necessary, die for their country, which was unlike any other fighting force in Europe. Napoleon discovered that the internal motivation generated from badges, purpose, and honor was stronger than external motivation from money, stock, and incentives.

All people want to live their lives with a purpose. A purpose-driven life has meaning. It has relevance. Nobody wants to take up space, eat, drink, and die. Everybody wants to leave something behind, to make a mark.

Purpose

The difference between leadership and management is purpose.

The happiest people on earth are those that have meaning and relevance to their life.

The difference between leadership and management is purpose. The happiest people on earth are those who have meaning and relevance to their lives.

You have to develop a team that wants to play for you, work hard for your vision, and work with meaning and purpose. As the old saying goes, the fish rots from the head down. You are the head. Your corporate culture is only a reflection of you. If you make a horrible product or service, if you lie and cheat on your taxes, if you don't refund customers' money, all that reflects on you. The easiest way to be successful is to live with integrity and purpose.

In 2012, a Deloitte's Shift Index survey found that 80 percent of people are dissatisfied with their jobs. Most people think of their jobs as work because they have to *work*—to exert the kind of forced effort that is the antithesis of *play*. There are some people who tolerate it and others who downright loathe it. They do their time, clocking in at eight in the morning and clocking out at five in the afternoon. They give the company their time in exchange for cash. It can be a miserable situation for both the employer and the employee. There's little passion or enjoyment.

The other 20 percent of Americans love their jobs for one reason: purpose.

The really fortunate people—all of the people on my team and me, for instance—actually love to work. Except we don't call it "work." I've never considered my vocation to be "work." It's my life! I have found that in order to be successful, I have to find these people who love to come to work. These people have a positive attitude, are proactive about implementing new systems in the office, are motivated to set goals and keep the rest of the team accountable to achieve those goals. They're the types of people who will stay overtime, just because it's what they'd rather be doing.

For example, in my practice, if I hired a receptionist who wanted to implement a good financial policy (like getting our patients to pay for their treatment up front instead of having to continually chase them down after their dental work is complete), she might call up other dental offices and ask their front desk staff what is working in their practices. She would network. She would get on the Internet and use my dental networking community site to see what others have found to be successful. And she would do all of this without my constant supervision, so that I can do what I'm supposed to be doing like a filling or a root canal.

It is critically important to staff to feel a sense of purpose in the work they do and to feel a sense of appreciation, both internally and externally from customers, co-workers, and management.

According to the United States Department of Labor, 26.3 percent of Americans volunteer. You know what this tells me? It tells me twenty-six of every hundred people are willing to work for free just to have meaning and purpose in their lives.

My assistant, Jan, often tells me about how her job has given her so much meaning and purpose. She fights the good fight; she takes the complex dental knowledge she has mastered and gets patients to listen to her, because they know if they do, they're going to keep their teeth for a lifetime. With this knowledge, they'll go home and start brushing and flossing as though they were powered by rocket fuel! If they do what Jan says, they're not going to learn things the hard way by waking up in the middle of the night with a toothache or losing all their teeth.

Don't gag your employees. Let them teach your customers. The word "doctor" comes from the Latin word "docere" which means, "to teach." Every employee who teaches is a doctor!

I'd say in about half of the dental offices in America, the dysfunction is palpable enough to cut through with a handpiece. It all stems from the top, doc. The dentist might be the only one in the practice who went to dental school, but he or she can't be the only "teacher" in the practice. As a dentist, you maybe have three operatories, but there's only one of you. You can't teach to everyone all the time!

As a business owner, delegate your teaching responsibilities. Empower your staff! Great teachers take the incredibly complex and make it so simple to understand that they empower all who listen. My hygienist knows what's going on in a patient's mouth. She knows what she sees on the X-ray. She can point out all of the trouble spots to the patient. My receptionist is the front line to my practice, and she should be able to share as much information as she knows with patients and potential patients over the phone.

When I ask a simple question of someone at a company and the response is, "Oh, I need to refer you to someone in sales," I think, *Really? You need someone in sales to answer my question? This is where you work! You work here all day long!* How does this person not know what's going on in his company enough to answer a simple question and not have to refer to another department? I swear all of the companies in America could replace 10 percent of their employees with a rubber plant.

As the leader of a company, you have to allow your people to find their purpose. Maybe their purpose is working for *you*! So let them *work*! Give them a longer leash. On the other hand, maybe their purpose is to go do something else. Working for you at least gives them the opportunity to give it the old "college try" before moving on to something else. If they're not working out, it's up to you to check this opportunity off of their list and give them the chance to go try something else.

ACTION POINTS

- Define the purpose of your business.
- Clarify your purpose and your core values with a clear, succinct mission statement that can fit on a 5 x 7 index card. If you can't explain what you do in a paragraph on an index card, I assure you no one in your company knows what your mission is and neither do your customers.
- Give your staff purpose to inspire top performance.

The purpose of life is not to be happy, but to matter, to be productive, to be useful, to have it make some difference that you have lived at all.

—Leo Rosten

Goals

When I began my media company for the dental profession, my goal was to connect every dentist around the world via the Internet so that no dentist would ever have to practice solo again. Dentistry is a cottage industry and many dentists practice alone. It's hard to practice dentistry alone in your little corner of the world. I noticed the best interactions between dentists did not occur during formal presentations at dental conferences, but outside the meetings, over a drink or hanging out by the pool. That's when they could really exchange stories about difficult cases or interesting patients who came through their doors. They were great conversations, but they were too infrequent. I wanted those discussions to happen in a closed forum online, so I decided to start my own website. I wanted my site to be a functional site where a community of dental professionals could flourish and raise the bar for dentistry as a whole.

Back in 1998, I was such a huge fan of Microsoft that we based our message boards off of their system. The problem was we weren't getting much action on the boards. We got a lot of complaints; it wasn't intuitive enough. It was a general pain, but I thought it was the most popular model for message boards at the time. That is, until I walked into work one day and saw one of my programmers checking out the message boards on ESPN. I asked him about the differences and he showed me. The interface was so easy and intuitive. You didn't need instructions to figure out how to post a comment in a thread. It was awesome. Right then and there we decided to scrap the direction we were headed and went with a new platform.

We adhered to our original goal, but tweaked it. Every day since, we have asked ourselves whether we are sticking with our goals and whether they should still be our goals.

In order to run a successful business, you need to have more than just a personality that is wired for business. You need appropriate and powerful goals.

You can't drive your business without goals or direction, much like you can't drive a car without a steering wheel. The tricky part is developing these goals—goals that will sustain your company both short term and long term. In 2010 the Annual Staples National Small Business Survey indicated 80 percent of the three hundred small businesses surveyed didn't keep track of their business goals. Seventy-seven percent said they hadn't even met their vision of the company. Why is that? I mean, if you think about it, isn't it amazing these businesses are still afloat? Is it possible that these small businesses have set the wrong goals for themselves?

Most businesses starting out will try to follow a certain business plan with certain goals in mind, but most of the time those efforts prove to be fruitless. You must be able to change your goals to fit the circumstances, and circumstances are changing all the time. You must be able to switch directions and alter your goals so that you can realistically achieve them.

Building an online community was only one of our goals. Our other goals were a lot broader, and a lot more personal.

You need to set goals for your business and for you personally. Consider which of these personal goals is most important to you:

- To improve the lives of your fellow man
- To become a pillar of your community
- To earn a spot on the board of a larger company
- To get rich

Surely we're all in business for personal reasons—selfish or unselfish. Otherwise what's the real purpose of running a business at all?

FOCUS ON THE FOUR B'S

I align the goals I set for my business with the goals I have set for my life. I like to focus on my four Bs: Body, Babe, Babies, and Business.

BODY

I remember coming home after a lousy day at school, and when I told my mom about it, the best she could come up with was, "At least you have your health." Here I was looking for constructive advice and what I got was a total cop out. At least, that's what I thought then. But as I got older I started to appreciate the wisdom in it. Without your body— without your health—what do you have? You can't do anything in this life if you're dying or dead. You have to take care of yourself.

The Dalai Lama was once asked what surprises him the most. He responded: "Man, because he sacrifices his health in order to make money. Then he sacrifices money to recuperate his health. And then he is so anxious about the future that he does not enjoy the present; the result being that he does not live in the present or the future; he lives as if he is never going to die, and then he dies having never really lived."

Sad, but all too true.

You need to keep your game together! I know we all can get off track, skipping meals and drinking seven-hundred-calorie coffee drinks in the morning and putting off exercise, even though we've been saying we're going to take off those extra twenty pounds one of these days. It can be easy to get stressed out and, instead of going for a run or going home and talking with a spouse, to go out for happy hour, smoke, drink and eat fatty, salty foods, only to feel like garbage the next day.

"What fits your busy schedule better, exercising one hour a day or being dead 24 hours a day?"

You have to remember: success is a marathon, not a sprint. The healthiest, most successful people get up every day and take care of their body first. Your body is your vehicle through life. The minute you start letting your body run out of gas or let it overheat, it is going to break down and you'll be going nowhere! My mom was right; at least you have your health, because without it, you have nothing!

The best decision I make every day is at 5:30 in the morning when I get up and work out my body for one hour. Contrary to popular belief, it doesn't matter what you do—just do *something* for an hour. If you hate jogging, try weightlifting, Pilates, Zumba, P90X, or Insanity—I love them all! I know that one of the best business decisions I can make is to make sure I'm still around for another twenty-five or thirty years, so I can keep working on my business.

I often think about the popular book series beginning with *The Girl with the Dragon Tattoo* by Swedish journalist and author Stieg Larsson. He gave the world an incredible trilogy, but from what we understand,

Larsson was working on a fourth book and had planned on so many more. According to an article about Larsson in *Rolling Stone*, a sickly Larsson and a friend entered the lobby of the magazine *Expo*, where Larsson was editor. Instead of waiting for the elevator, Larsson elected to take the stairs, even though his friend noticed he did not look well. He was facing a pretty brutal deadline and needed to get the next issue out the door. By the time he reached the *Expo* offices, it was too late. He had suffered a severe heart attack.

Larsson never exercised, worked in a high-stress job, ate nothing but processed junk food, and smoked like a chimney. It is no wonder his heart gave out. It is unfortunate that his untimely death stole Larsson away from the world, as well as the future adventures of characters such as Mikael Blomkvist and Lisbeth Salander. For fans of the series, there will always remain a "what if?"

Too many artists have left us wondering "what if?" Elvis Presley, Karen Carpenter, Kurt Cobain, Jimi Hendrix, Janis Joplin, Michael Jackson, Chris Farley, John Belushi, Jim Morrison, Whitney Houston . . . the list goes on and on.

You're never too busy to take care of your body first.

BABE

I'm not going to delve too deep into marital or relationship issues. That's a whole other book—one I'm not going to write. But you definitely need the support of your "babe"—your lover, your partner, your soul mate. You need to strike a definitive balance between your professional life and your personal one. One of my company's twelve core values says as much, and it's important to be fully present in both.

As you develop your business and personal goals, you have to include your babe. If you are married, your spouse is your most important business partner, whether you acknowledge it or not. In community property states, your spouse actually owns half of what you own anyway. Nothing destroys a business faster than discord with your babe. So make sure you consider your relationship with your babe as you determine your personal and business goals.

Here's the thing: for those of you who would much rather read a book on management or business than go see a special anniversary screening of *When Harry Met Sally*, remember the importance of remaining fully present in your personal life as well. Go to the movies with your spouse. Go see some sporting event. If you're like me and you catch your mind wandering rather than enjoying a movie, stop yourself. Allow yourself to get into it. Besides, the interpersonal relationships that you're watching up there on screen are great human resources (HR) training!

To determine the goals for your marriage and/or relationship, you have to know whether your spouse has the personality to live with a businessperson. Some spouses or significant others seek the security of a steady income from a steady job. Going into business for yourself is mired in uncertainty. I've seen marriages crumble under the pressure. You need your spouse's full support.

Between the two of you, you have to decide how much time you need to spend together, how to divide household responsibilities, and how you envision the future. All have an impact on your business and your business impacts all of them.

BABIES

My four boys never asked to be born. I wanted them, therefore I feel totally responsible for them. They take a lot of time, patience, and money, and they are the four most important people in my life. When I was seventeen and moved an eight-hour drive away from my family in Wichita, Kansas, to go to college in Omaha, Nebraska, I hardly ever got to talk to or see my parents except for breaks. Now, with smartphones, texting, and email, the first thing I do every single morning is text my boys. I call them all the time. I fly out to see my oldest son and his family or fly him to see me at least four times a year. He calls me when he gets off work. We talk for hours . . . still! My babies are everything to me.

Judith Wells Brickner (Howard's ex-wife), Zach,
Ryan, Greg, Eric, and Howard Farran

Eric, Greg, Zach, and Ryan Farran
in 1995

Again, you must align your business goals with your relationship to your babies. You have to arrange your business to allow the time you feel you need to raise your kids properly—to meet their physical, emotional, and financial needs.

BUSINESS

What is your business?

Are you the pastry shop with the signature éclairs? Are you the best cosmetic dentist in town? Are you the state's best-known, low-cost used auto dealer? *Clearly define your product or service.*

Abraham Maslow identified five levels of human needs in a hierarchy beginning with *physiological* (health, food, sleep); *safety* (shelter, removal from danger); *love and belonging* (affection, family, relationship); *esteem* (self-esteem, achievement, respect of and by others), and *self-actualization* (creativity, problem solving, lack of prejudice, self-fulfillment). Every business has to make something that satisfies at least one basic human need. If you're making doughnuts, you're meeting the physiological need for food. If you're Facebook founder Mark Zuckerberg, you're meeting the need for belonging. If you're running a gym, you're meeting the physiological need for health and perhaps also for self-fulfillment.

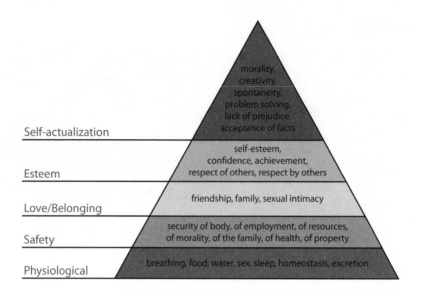

If someone asks what need your business fills for your customers and you say, "all of them," you won't be in business much longer. Imagine a gym that sells you doughnuts while you're on the treadmill. If you try to be everything to everyone, you'll end up being nothing to anyone.

Satisfying a need isn't enough, however. Jack Welch, who ran General Electric, said if you're not number one, number two, or number three in your category, you had better retool and fix what it is you're doing or you might as well just get out of the business altogether. Either sell it or close it down. Hopefully, if you sell it, the person buying it will have a better idea.

If you can't be in the top three, you had better be unique. Your customers want what is unique about your product or service. This is what we call your unique selling proposition (USP).

All dental practices are not the same. Neither are all law practices, muffler shops, or software companies. Think about all of the sandwich franchises out there: Subway, Jimmy John's, Quiznos, Charley's, Panera Bread, Paradise Bakery, Firehouse Subs, Extreme Pita, Jersey Mike's— the list goes on and on. Is any single one of those franchises just like the next? No way! Sure, they all offer pretty much the same thing— sandwiches—but Subway wants you to "eat fresh" and makes the food in front of you. Others prepare them in a kitchen while you wait. The mission of Jimmy John's is to hook you up with your fresh-made sandwich with a wicked quickness, while Panera Bread wants you to relax and enjoy a leisurely meal in their comfortable environment. Not one company is a copycat of another, even within its own milieu.

The name of my business, my brand—Today's Dental—is something easy to remember. Some businesses have crazy names that no one can remember. Your name should explain your product or your service. You may be in love with your name because you got it from your parents, but that's an emotional decision, not a business decision. If you're looking for a dentist and you see a sign that reads "Today's Dental," you're likely to remember that. Which is why I don't call my practice "Howard Farran, DDS."

In dentistry, we deliver good teeth. But if all a dentist does is X-rays, cleanings, exams, fillings, and crowns, she will have a difficult time achieving a million-dollar practice. You have to differentiate yourself with price, quality or service (more on that later), and continually upgrade your services to increase your market share and meet demand.

That said, the only way to beat the competition is to work harder than they do. There's no substitute for hard work. How many of your competitors are working as hard as they can? I venture to say, not many! The best way to succeed is to try to out-work everyone else. It's also the easiest, because you'll be the only one trying!

Choose the Right Location

Once you've defined your business, the most important decision you need to make is this: Where do you want to live?

Bottom line: you can move to a city that is good for business, or you can set up a business where you live. You need to decide which you wish to do.

Over the years, many people have told me that I am one lucky guy, because I opened up my dental office in a booming area of Phoenix called Ahwatukee. I opened up my dental office in 1987 when Ahwatukee had roughly 25,000 people living there. By the time my office was twenty-five years old, Ahwatukee had bloomed to more than 75,000 residents. I still hear how lucky I am.

It had nothing to do with luck and here's why.

Back when I was teenager visiting dental practices in my hometown, I heard dentists repeat some version of, "That dental school in Kansas City keeps pumping out more than a hundred new docs every year and many come back to Wichita, saturating the market, so now I have to do battle with more competition in an area that isn't increasing in population." Every year in Wichita, dentists were finding it more difficult to make a living.

I thought about this a lot through four years of high school, three years of undergrad, and four years of dental school. I thought, "What's the point in going through all this schooling if I'm going to practice in an area where the odds are against me?"

So what did I do?

I requested information from the federal department of economic security and I found out that between 1985 and 2000, this department anticipated that the U.S. would create thirty million new jobs, half of which would be in five metropolitan areas: Tampa, Boston, Phoenix, Silicon Valley and Orange County, CA. I didn't want to move to Florida because I don't like humidity. I didn't want to move to Boston because I was tired of cold and snowy winters. California, in the mind of this sheltered Kansas boy, was all drugs, sex, and rock & roll. So that left Phoenix. Remember, my mother had always pointed out how Mr. Sun was always shining over Arizona in the weather reports.

I did my research. I studied census, transportation, and utility data. I could see which areas were experiencing explosive growth and which areas were flat or contracting.

I can remember looking at my map and seeing that in this one corner of Tempe, Arizona, there were twenty-eight dentists, even though the population in that zip code had shrunk in the past decade. I remember thinking to myself, "What in the world was the twenty-eighth dentist thinking when he moved in there?" I've never seen twenty-eight McDonald's restaurants on a single corner.

Too many business people choose a location without any data, without any measurements. Without ever having set foot in Phoenix, I already knew the area in which I planned to set up my practice.

So when people say that I was "lucky" because I moved a thousand miles away to Phoenix in 1987 without ever having been to this town, I know better. I made my own luck, and you can, too!

The best marketing is a winning team in a prime location.

My dental practice, Today's Dental, is housed in a standalone signature building on the corner of 48th Street and Elliot where everyone can see it.

My office is near a big four-way intersection, next to a big Safeway store, Chase bank, pizzeria, tanning salon, Walgreen's pharmacy—all in a busy plaza where no one in the community can miss seeing Today's Dental. Everybody knows we're there! We're even one of the few dental practices in the area that you can see at night.

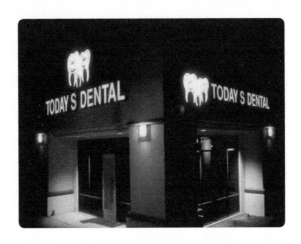

I recently had some long conversations with two despondent dentists. They are both from a town of 5,000 residents, and the only factory in town—which employed all of the townsfolk—closed down a year ago. The town is drying up and 80 percent of their insured patients were people who worked at that factory. Now those people are not only unemployed, they are leaving the city because there are no job opportunities in town, they have no money, and they need to downsize. I listened to these two doctors tell me they were born in that town, married in that town, and had children in that town.

I told them it was time to make a tough decision. I told them they needed to move, plain and simple. I said, "Look at your ancestors. They left almost everything they had behind for the opportunity to have a better life in America—that is, if they survived. And you are afraid to leave what is fast becoming a ghost town for another city or state with better economic stability?"

If you've currently set up shop in a depreciating area, can you move to a better area nearby? What would be the costs? What would you lose? What would you *gain*?

If you know where you want to live, you feel good about your body, you have a healthy, functional, productive relationship with your babies and your babe, then you can attack your business and, like the Army says, be all you can be.

ACTION POINTS

- List your goals for your body, your health.
- If you are married, list your goals for your marriage, for building a successful relationship with your partner.
- If you are a parent, list your goals for your babies. Make time, plans, and budgets for your family, and don't forget the life insurance.
- Define your product or service. What is your business? What is your unique selling proposition (USP)? What makes your business different?
- Identity the need your business fulfills on a single 5 x 7 index card.
- Decide where you want to live and locate your business. Research the economics of any area you consider. What is the population? What is your population's median income? How has the population changed over the past five to ten years? Are people moving into your area or are they leaving for greener pastures? Remember: business, in three words, is *supply and demand*. Are people demanding what you're supplying?

- What about the town itself? Are they building anything new? Is the infrastructure—roads, bridges, utilities—expanding? Are other new companies moving in? Identify what makes your business unique.
- What can you do to differentiate your business from the competition in your area?

*We all die. The goal isn't to live forever,
the goal is to create something that will.*

—*Chuck Palahniuk*, Diary

5

Know Your Employees

"The customer is always right." Right?

Wrong!

Your employees come first, not your customers. If some customer abuses your team and you stand behind the jerk, your team will become completely demoralized, because they know you will never have their back.

When it comes to building a winning team, the name of the game is *loyalty*. What are you doing to ensure your team consists of reliable people you believe in and who believe in you and your business? Do your employees know your story? Do they know why you started this business? Do you *ever* let them know how important they are to your business and how much you value them?

In order to have a winning team, you need to create it! Here's how.

HO THE RIGHT PLAYERS ARE
IR TEAM

In sports you want the best athletes—the ones who can consistently get the job done and win the game for the team. You want the same thing for your business, a winning team. As in sports, you need to build a team of top performers with complementary skills to create a winning business. The most important thing your team has to deliver is quality, and quality equals consistency.

You need employees who will deliver the vision you have defined for your business. If someone doesn't get my corporate culture, doesn't embrace our core values, then I'm going to show that person the door. As part of our core values, we require our teams to "be passionate, enthusiastic, and determined to make a difference." Try as you might, you can't train someone to be any one of those things, so you must make sure you're hiring people who carry these traits and be prepared to jettison those who do not.

The Pareto principle (named after Italian economist Vilfredo Pareto and also known as the 80/20 rule) appears routinely in science, business, and life. The rule states that where a large number of factors are involved, 20 percent of those factors contribute to 80 percent of the result. It is a common rule of thumb in business, for example, that 80 percent of your sales come from 20 percent of your customers.

Since the Deloitte's Shift Index survey indicates that 80 percent of people hate their jobs, it stands to reason that if you want to be a successful millionaire, you and your employees have to be among the 20 percent who love their jobs.

I believe employees can be divided into increments A through F, like grades in school. Employees who exude a positive attitude even during tough times, are passionate about what they do, and have a strong intellectual curiosity, all fall into the A and B player category. Those who find work dissatisfying and always have an excuse as to why things went wrong fall into the C, D, or F category.

Think of A through F players in terms of a basketball team. If the ball goes out of bounds, the A player is going to dive for it, even if it means hurting herself or falling on the ground to save it. The B players are there to catch the ball when it is thrown in bounds. They are good back up—not necessarily leaders, but good, reliable workers. C players always drag the whole team down, but often fly under the radar, making them the most difficult to identify and get rid of. D and F players are the ones who walk, instead of run, up and down the court. They don't block shots and they don't shoot baskets. They're not good for the team. But they're always the easiest to identify and fire.

HIRE THE RIGHT PEOPLE

The interview process is *serious business*; if you want to be successful, you have to learn how to win that part of the game.

If you own a home, how many houses did you look at before you committed your dollars? If you are married, how many people did you date before you proposed to that special person? Ten? Twenty? I can't tell you enough: hiring the right employee is *that* important. You want to hire people who will stay with you for life.

I find it insane when a business advertises an opening in the newspaper or online and then quickly hires one of the first three people to drop off a resume. That's nuts. Do you really think the New York Yankees would interview only three people for a catcher position? Or do you think they might actually scout out every single catcher playing for a university today? The Yankees take HR extremely seriously.

In my business we often spend up to two months on the hiring process. We know that if we get it right, we may have a player for ten to twenty-five years.

When you're hiring, you'll likely receive a wide array of resumes. Some will have the full range of experience you'd expect from an applicant, others might have some, and the rest will be among those who send out a resume because any job will do. Like people, you're going to receive resumes that range from A to F. If a magician is applying for an engineering position, the likelihood of that resume disappearing into your wastebasket is pretty good.

Once we've whittled the list down to a smaller pool of applicants (those with relevant skills, job experience, great references, good examples of previous employment, etc.), we like to talk to them over the phone to get to know their personalities. A person might look amazing on paper, but if they have zero personality over the phone, we won't even ask them to come in for a personal interview. If we like what we hear over the phone, the next step is to invite them to come in for the initial interview.

The hardest part of the HR process is trying to identify the star players via a one-hour interview. This is why I recommend a multiple-step interview process that involves the entire management team. If you hire someone who doesn't jibe with the rest of your team, you've wasted a lot of time and resources in getting that person up to speed, and it hurts to have to start the hiring process over. I always have my entire management team interview the applicants as well, often when I'm not in the room, so they can give me their honest and independent thoughts about the person, and to give the applicant the opportunity to ask questions of those on the front line.

Here are some questions we might ask in the latter stages of the interview process:

- Why did you leave, or why are you leaving your previous employer?
- What did you like about your last job?
- What did you like the least about your last job?
- What would you change about your last job?
- What wouldn't you change about your last job?
- What were your responsibilities at your previous employer? What is your greatest strength that will benefit you in this position?
- What do you enjoy doing most in your line of work?
- Why did you choose this field?
- How flexible are you with coming in early or staying late when needed?

- How do you make customers feel special and cared for?
- What are your salary requirements?
- Why do you want to work for our company?

Obviously, until the new employee actually starts working in your business you won't really know whether he will work out. The founder of Southwest Airlines, Herb Kelleher, always said, "You should *always* hire on attitude and train for skills." You can train a star player for the position but you can't change someone's personality. Skill set is important if vital to the job (you wouldn't hire an engineer who didn't have a diploma), but attitude is the key ingredient in a great new hire. Attitude always determines your altitude.

Rather than spending everyone's time trying to motivate one employee, I am going to hire one who is already internally motivated. I am not going to put it on myself to come up with all of the big ideas; I am going to find an employee who comes up with their own big ideas. This is what George Steinbrenner taught us all. If a pitcher didn't work out on the Yankees, Steinbrenner didn't send him to pitching school, he fired the pitcher and found a better one.

Some people have great instincts for hiring others. Some do not. If the last several people you hired were let go a year or so into their tenure at your company, chances are you're not good at bringing on new people. Granted, nobody in the world gets hiring right all the time. It's impossible. But if the last five people you hired left on their own volition because of an issue within the company, or if you had to let them go for some reason, your hiring skills might not be as solid as you think. You need to realize this. You need to own up to it. And you need to stop right away and delegate this responsibility to someone who can actually bring the best people to you and your team. Being short an employee at any company can be excruciating, but not as much as having the *wrong* person on the team.

In all Fortune 500 companies, HR is a specialty just like accounting, finance, engineering, operations and logistics, and supply chain management. In the first ten years of owning my business, I did all the interviewing for the initial "weed out," and then I would introduce them to the management team. At five years, I achieved a success rate of about 50 percent. When I hired my current media company president, Lorie Xelowski, I quickly realized she was far better at hiring and put her in charge of HR. I estimate her success rate at close to 90 percent.

As a CEO, it's more important to know what you are *not* good at than what you are. Most people know what they're good at, but most people don't focus enough on realizing what they're not good at, and that's what a team is for. Your team is supposed to support you. I tell people, "If you don't like looking at your numbers, then you can't outsource all your books to an accounting firm. You need to bring a bookkeeper in house who is there living the numbers forty hours a week, fifty-two weeks a year." If you're not good at HR, maybe your spouse or someone else on your management team is. Delegate.

Entrepreneurial Curve

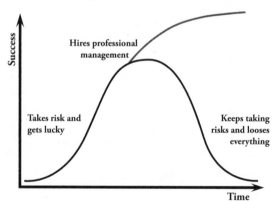

Time

MOST entrepreneurs are good at vision and risk taking. In the typical entrepreneurial curve, an entrepreneur (after an initial dip) takes off like a rocket, only to splash down in the ocean five years later. Recent research conducted by the Small Business Administration indicates that a third of businesses fail within the first two years. The most successful entrepreneurs are those who develop a management team made up of strong players who complement the risk-taking entrepreneur with vision in all the areas the entrepreneur is either A) not interested in, or B) simply not good at.

In your business, you manage three things: People, Time, and Money. When it comes to the people component, HR is critical. If you aren't good at it, find someone who is.

If you aren't good at watching the numbers, hire one or more good, full-time, in-office bookkeepers.

If you aren't good at time management, well . . . you need to get good at it, but we'll cover that in Part Two.

Hiring the Right People
Lorie Xelowski

I started working for Howard Farran back in 1998—not in a management position, but rather in handling all of the daily and monthly accounting tasks. I had no idea what an amazing ride I was in for, or how much my role was going to change over the next fifteen years!

Within the first two years, I transitioned into the general manager position. Having worked for the past twenty years on the accounting side of things, I quickly realized accounting is much easier than managing people! In my opinion, finding the right team is THE most important component of a successful business. Without the right people, you can't accomplish your goals or take your company to the next level.

During the hiring process, I do things a bit differently than most. Many consultants will tell you that having prepared interview questions is key, and that the right interview questions are critical to finding the right fit. My style has always been to interview off the cuff, listen to my gut, and get to know that person during the process. Depending on the position, I like to have at least two, if not three, interviews and include the management team, as well as the team that will be working with this person.

The initial interview is to get to know them, review their resume, learn about their previous work experience, and get an initial first impression. We then narrow down the candidates to the two or three who made the best first impression without bringing up any red flags (based on the interview questions listed earlier).

The next round is more informal, including several team members. Often we schedule it as a lunch interview in a restaurant. That way we get to see the person in a more casual environment, get to know them better and, again, look for any red flags.

However, the outcome is never guaranteed. I have experienced a handful of times when the candidate interviewed with flying colors, only to completely disappoint once they started doing the job. In a few cases the problem wasn't even detectable until *after* the ninety-day probationary period. Humans are complex, so you never really know if someone is going to work out until they start the job; even then it sometimes takes a while to know if they are the right fit.

Corporate culture is everything. When you build a team of hard working, functional people, those that don't fit it in with that culture typically stand out like a sore thumb! Lazy or dysfunctional personalities—those who would rather surf the Internet than work, who love to gossip, or are "drama queens"—very quickly become uncomfortable around the functional, hard-working people in your office.

On rare occasion you might hire someone who isn't a star player but who's very good at hiding it. This is the worst type of employee, the kind that eventually becomes a virus in your organization. It is critical that you identify these individuals as quickly as possible, because they can tear down what was once a great culture; they can divide teams and departments before you realize what has happened.

When it does become apparent they are not the right fit, or worse, have done damage to your organization, immediately call attention to their dysfunctional behavior. Give them the opportunity to change, but if they can't change within a short period of time, then you need to move as quickly as possible to replace them. As a manager, it is always easier to ignore problems than to tackle them head on, but if you strive to be the best manager/leader you can possibly be, you must continuously address the issues and tweak your team.

The HR process is continually evolving and changing. It is valuable to hone your hiring skills, because switching out staff is expensive and time consuming. Hiring the right person for each position is critical to the overall growth and success of your company. I believe you should hire for attitude and train for the skills necessary. If you find people who have a great attitude—who are humble, hungry and smart—I don't think you can ever go wrong. Education and skill set are never as important to me as inherent traits—those traits that are key to a healthy corporate culture and taking your company to the next level!

EVALUATE EACH EMPLOYEE'S PERFORMANCE OBJECTIVELY

When I started practicing dentistry and an employee of mine wasn't performing up to par, I thought it was because of me. I thought I needed to possess genuine leadership abilities and charisma in order to manage and motivate my team. I took complete ownership of my employees' behavior and output. I even went to great lengths to change *myself* so my team could perform better. I thought it was up to me to motivate them to do the best job they could. What I learned from George Steinbrenner is if you employ a pitcher who can't pitch, you don't go down to the dugout and motivate the guy, you don't take him to dinner for a pep talk or send him to pitching school—you fire him and find a better pitcher.

Steinbrenner's example corrected my number-one business fallacy: You don't manage people; you manage the HR process of *attracting and retaining the best people.* I have more than fifty employees. Every quarter, Lorie and I go through that list of employees the same way Steinbrenner would look at his roster, and ask: "Is this person a good employee? Is this person a team player? Does he or she play nice in the sandbox? Is this person honest? Does this person have integrity? Is this person one of my brightest employees? Is this employee internally motivated? Is this employee diving for the ball? Is this employee hitting homeruns? Are any of our employees consistently breaking our core values?"

Everyone has bad days. Some people can get off their games, and they need a little time to readjust. But when they're *often* off their game, that's when you have a problem. I firmly believe that if you fire someone and they're shocked, you're not only a bad manager, you're a bad person. That is why the review process and the immediate attention to issues head on are so important.

In my opinion, the idea that the only things that matter are profit and shareholders is absolute garbage. It takes a community to run a business. You wouldn't even have your business without a community behind it.

When an employee is burned out and unmotivated to do his job, lots of managers think: "I need to motivate this person. I need to be a leader. I need to encourage this person. It's all my fault."

That's not true. The truth is that you can't manage your employees' lives; you can only manage your team roster.

I've heard office managers say things like, "Oh, I can't get rid of her. She's been here for ten years." This is wrong! Be like George Steinbrenner! He'd say: "I don't care how long you've been with the team. What are you doing for me *now*?!" Steinbrenner hired and fired plenty of managers because of their worth to the team. How worthy are your staff members of being on a championship team? Remember, every single player contributes to winning or losing the game; there's no such thing as a neutral player.

Hire the people you not only want to hire, but *need* to hire. Build the team that's going to make your business the most successful business in the world. If Steinbrenner wanted to make the World Series every year, he needed the best players on his team. If you want to run a successful business, you need the best players on *your* team.

Don't tolerate a mediocre staff. If you want to have a successful business, you need a team full of A players at the top of their game. George Steinbrenner would be the first to tell you that the best players don't come cheap. You get what you pay for, so be sure you set your wages to match the high quality of your employees.

KEEP THE RIGHT PEOPLE

I have learned a lot of tough lessons living in Phoenix, Arizona. For example I've learned that keeping the best people on your staff isn't always up to you. I've hired young people who came from the Northeast or the Midwest because they "always wanted to live in the desert," or "wanted to get out of the horrible winters." But as soon as they got married and had their first child, what's the first thing they wanted to do? Move back home to be close to their parents and friends.

There also have been instances when I've hired someone I considered top notch and would have loved to keep for decades, but because their spouse was in the military or took a job elsewhere, they had to leave. Those circumstances can be painful for you and your business, but they happen. When staff does leave, it's up to you to hire the same high caliber person—not simply fill the spot with the first temp who comes along. As I said, I take the interview process for potential new staff as seriously as I would in choosing a spouse.

Keeping great staff requires the same skill set as keeping a spouse. If you have been married five times and your average employee leaves after two years, then you shouldn't be shocked to discover 80 percent of your customers have left, too. It's time to begin honing better people skills. People skills—whether with your spouse and kids, or with your staff and customers—are the most important skills you can wish for. (I recommend that everyone in business take a Dale Carnegie training course to develop better interpersonal skills.)

A lot of people who have high staff turnover have benefited greatly from counseling. I'm serious! Just as a marriage counselor can help you to keep your marriage, a counselor, therapist, or psychologist may help you unravel whatever you are doing to drive away staff and hurt your business.

To be an effective leader, you need to learn how to communicate and how to give praise. If you don't want to change or learn how to be an excellent manager, then you need to find someone who can handle *all* of that for you. Find an office manager or general manager who can take care of all of your daily HR duties. If you're not willing to change, find someone who can successfully recruit and retain your staff long term.

The Value of Long-Term Employees
Jan Sweeney, dental assistant

My parents always told me "when opportunity knocks, you answer," and I did just that on April 18, 1988, when I started working for Dr. Farran. I had worked as an assistant for a little more than six years, yet had no idea what was in store for me. He was a new dentist just out of school and starting a practice on his own. Working with Dr. Farran showed me how challenging dentistry can be and that facing challenges only makes you stronger. He taught me to not only like what I do, but love what I do.

I really do love what I do.

When you work at a business for a long period of time, you work and grow as a team. You learn together and reach your goals together. You become a family. The patients sense that. When they see a team member with a familiar face, they become more at ease.

It's exciting to get to know your patients in a personal way. You watch their kids grow up. When those kids start bringing their kids into the practice, you really start to feel old! All kidding aside, you grow with the practice and with the patients, and that's what makes an awesome team.

I treat all of my patients like family. We don't just talk about dental issues; we talk about life adventures. I learn so much from my patients.

Since more hours are spent at work than at home, I want to be around fun, positive people. Long-term employees who are positive and really love what they do are key to a successful practice/business.

FIRE THE RIGHT PEOPLE

Not everyone you hire is going to work out for you. Maybe you realize this immediately about an employee, or maybe not until years down the line. Remember, it's not a question about whether or not someone did a good job for you years ago, it's a matter of, "What are you doing for me now?"

If you listen closely to the coach of any professional sports team, the sole focus is on winning the next game. I'm a big proponent of moving someone from a position in which they're not excelling to something that might be more up their alley, but that usually only happens if there's a position to move that person into—and in a small business or your department of a Fortune 500 company, chances of that happening are pretty rare. Firing someone can be gut wrenching for some of us, unpleasant at best, but in order to keep your company moving forward, you need to know how to evaluate your team and jettison those who aren't doing what you want. It's not fair to your team to constantly lose games because the manager won't get rid of one of the players. No one is indispensable.

Everyone says they hire all A players, but that's pretty hard to do. Even when you believe you've just hired an A player, wait to see how it's going after ninety days. Still think that person's an A player?

You should be sharp enough never to hire a D or an F player (they make a lot of grunts and groans when you interview them). C players do their job but don't go the extra mile. They don't help with anything they are not explicitly told they need to do. An exceptional boss is one who can find the C players and extract them from the team.

The problem with C players is their behavior is not fair for the rest of the team. If I'm playing basketball and the ball is going out of bounds, I'm going to dive for it even if it means hurting myself to save it. However, if I throw the ball in, I'm expecting one of my teammates to recover the ball and go shoot a basket. If I dive for the ball but no one is around to catch it, I'm going to quit diving for the ball.

It's hard for the rest of the team because they end up picking up the slack for the other players. Here's a classic example:

The dentist usually leaves a few minutes before five, and the lazy assistant, a C player, who is supposed to prep for tomorrow's early morning patients, skirts out the backdoor just seconds after the doctor. She's clocked out; work will be there for her in the morning. The other assistant, an A player who usually sticks around for another half-hour, is thinking that tomorrow morning at eight o'clock the practice has three patients—one for the hygienist and two for the dentist. So she goes through to make sure all three operatories are set up and clean. When she is setting up one of the rooms for a crown seat, she notices the patient's crown isn't in the operatory, nor is it is the storage space where they are kept.

She calls the dental lab where crowns are made. At this point it's already a quarter past five; this is overtime that a person on salary is not getting paid for. The lab got the dates mixed up but offers to deliver it that night. The assistant is thinking: I need to do this for our patient and the lab person is ready to go home and have dinner with their spouse and children but, instead, is going to deliver this crown, all because the lazy assistant didn't do her job and take care of this earlier. Why is the lab doing this? Why am I doing this? Am I the only one who cares?

Anyone would get discouraged in a situation like this. And it doesn't take long for an A player to justify behaving like a B or C player because everyone else around her is behaving like one. Even though the lab offered to deliver the crown that evening, assistant A thinks about how the other assistant flew out at a quarter 'til but was paid until five o'clock. She thinks about how the dentist doesn't care because the dentist hasn't noticed her going the extra mile lately. She tells the lab guy: "Forget it. Go home and have dinner with your kids. This is crazy. We'll reschedule the patient." She wonders what will be said when the dentist walks in at eight the next morning. Assistant A goes home frustrated that evening because she's not playing on a winning team.

In the morning when assistant C comes in and announces the crown isn't there, the dentist simply tells her to reschedule rather than holding her accountable. If the dentist doesn't expect anything out of her employees and the A player isn't appreciated for her hard work, she's going to stop giving 110 percent or going the extra mile.

C players are the cancer of every organization. They rub off on the rest of the team and create a corporate culture of mediocrity. I call them energy vampires. They are subtle and they suck all the energy out of your business.

When you employ C players, they're trading their time for money. They don't care one iota about your business or your products or your customers. They're there because it allows them to earn a living in order to do what they truly want to do. It's likely they sit around all day just dreaming of what it is they're going to do the second they get out of work. You need to fire these people, not just because they're bringing down your business and your team, but also because they need to discover their true calling.

I had a dental assistant who looked decent on paper, but she only lasted on my team for about three months. I was pretty fresh out of dental school, and she was about ten years older than I and had been a dental assistant for about fifteen years. She had all the credentials needed to do the job. She was very proficient; I had very little concern with her ability to do the job. It's just that she wasn't a people person.

Perhaps you've been to a dentist's office where the assistant is poking around in your mouth asking you questions you can't possibly answer because your mouth is open and stuffed with gauze. Yet she keeps talking, telling you what she sees in your mouth, what problem areas you need to focus on, etc. That's the kind of assistant I want: someone who's so concerned about the current state of your teeth, she won't shut up about it.

Well, this particular assistant of mine didn't talk. She didn't talk to the patient or the rest of the staff. I'd watch her, puzzled. When she did talk to people, I couldn't believe *how* she talked to them. She had very little empathy for others—something I discussed with her several times.

We got along pretty well and I genuinely liked her as a person, but I knew I had to fire her. When it came time to meet with her and let her go, I first said, "You're being fired right now." (And by the way, if you have to fire someone, "You're being fired right now," needs to be the first thing out of your mouth. No story. No hemming and hawing.

You need to lay it all out from the get-go and say, "You're fired."). When she asked why, I told her what I had told her at her 90-day review: "You don't like people. You don't work well with people. In fact, I think you hate people. And you've been a dental assistant for fifteen years. You know what you need to do? You need to get out of dentistry! It's not for you! I really think you need to find a job where you're not working with people at all. You're not cut out for retail."

As I was saying this to her, I recalled the numerous conversations she and I had about her garden and her plants. She was really into it! She could list off what was in her garden, what it took to care for certain plants, which ones needed more sunlight than others . . . Whenever she spoke to me about plants, it was as though a light turned on in her eyes.

I told her, point blank: "You seriously need to get a job at a plant nursery. It's the only thing you ever talk about with any passion whatsoever, and I really think plants are the only thing on the planet that would actually get along with you!"

We settled everything pretty soon after that. She collected her belongings and I walked her to her car. Yes, she was disappointed that she was getting fired, but we had reached an understanding.

Six months later, guess who shows up at my practice for her six-month cleaning? You got it. I was very surprised to see her. In fact she came in with her husband and her kids. She sought me out right away. I didn't know if I was going to get punched or what. She shook my hand vigorously as she told me getting fired from my dental practice was the best thing that ever happened to her.

Seriously!

She told me she was completely trapped in thinking she had to keep doing what she was doing because dental assistants made pretty decent money. She had gone to school and spent all this time becoming a dental assistant, but never once stopped to ask herself whether she actually enjoyed it. She now worked for a plant nursery and *loved* it! She thanked me up and down for breaking her unfortunate momentum.

When an employee in your office is not involved—when they are detached—give them the freedom they need and fire them! Most people, when they're being fired, think the person doing the firing is a total jerk. No! Not true! If they loved their job, if this job gave them purpose, if it was the first thing they thought about when they woke up and the last thing they thought about when they went to bed, no one would *have* to fire them. They'd be doing a good job!

Humans are too complex to offer up any blanket statement on anything, but from my experience, if you have to fire a C player, it could be because they really don't like what they're doing—which means they're in the wrong career! It's almost like a divorce. There can be fighting going on and total dysfunction, but it finally takes one person to be decisive and say: "This can't go on forever. It's time to end this for both our sakes."

In the wise words of Albert Einstein: "Insanity is doing the same thing over and over and expecting different results."

When you fire a C player, it's not because you don't like the person, it's because they're just not right for the job they're currently doing. As twisted and crazy as it sounds at the outset, you're doing most C players a favor when you fire them.

I can't emphasize enough the following points:

- If you have your team's back, they will have yours and the company's.

- D and F players are easy to pick out. Be the BOSS and jettison them immediately. C players are hard to pick out, but you need to be wary of them, because C players bring down the morale of every hard-working team.

- Your job is not to motivate your employees. Always try to hire internally motivated people. Make sure they have the proper background and continual training for the position, but above all, hire the best attitude. You can always train for skill, but you can never train for attitude!

- If someone doesn't work out, fire them. They will be happier in the long run, and so will you and your team.

ACTION POINTS

- Make sure your employees come first, not your customers.
- Determine whether you have the right people on your team.
- Always try to hire A and B players.
- Review your staff's performance yearly, at 90 days for new employees, or when there are issues that need to be addressed.
- Do what it takes to retain the right people.
- Fire the right people. It's easy to spot the Ds and the Fs. It's the C players who are killing your company!

Employees are your most valuable assets.
They are the heart and guts of a company.

—Carlos Ghosn

Trust and Respect

THAT'S THE STUPIDEST IDEA I EVER HEARD!

In 2008, when I told my office I decided to buy a $125,000 CEREC CAD/CAM machine that makes crowns in our office in about an hour, my long-term assistant, Jan, who has been with me for twenty-five years, blurted out, "That is the stupidest idea I've ever heard."

So I asked her, "Why?" Jan, knowing she can speak freely and knowing that she's not going to get fired for disagreeing with me, said: "Are you kidding me? This place has not been remodeled since 1994! Our office desperately needs a makeover. I've already looked into that and it's going to run us about $50,000 to $75,000."

Then my office manager, Sandy—who has been with me for fifteen years—chimed in and said: "Since this recession hit, the last thing we need is a CAD/CAM machine. What we need are new patients. We need a marketing program."

Sandy had already looked into a marketing firm that specializes in marketing for the dental industry, New Patients, Inc., and obtained a proposal.

nth of team discussions, we figured out a way to do all
)deled our office, signed on with the marketing firm, *and*
purchased a CAD/CAM machine.

One of the biggest signs of trust is that all of your employees can argue with you freely, out loud, and feel safe. That's even one of my company's core values: *Strive to make everyone feel safe, valued, and important.*

That begins and ends with trust and respect.

Trust and respect are two business concepts that too often get left out of business school curriculum. We get so busy talking about cash flow, shareholder value, and meeting the bottom line that, most of the time, the idea of treating staff well gets put on the back burner. But here's the thing: if you want to have cash flow and you want to meet your bottom line, you need happy employees. This is where trust and respect come in and why I believe they warrant an entire chapter.

You wouldn't turn your eye to someone getting robbed, but you're going to let people in your company get emotionally abused? Don't ever tolerate employees saying bad things about others in your company. People aren't going to have fun, or be passionate and enthusiastic, when they have to spend every waking minute with the office jerk. Humans are very emotional and complex, and they are very sensitive. If they're not respected they're not going to give you their best performance, and they might not even want to continue working for you.

The Importance of a Positive and Respectful Workplace
By Marcie Donavon, circulation director

Like so many people, I spend most of my waking hours—a large percentage of my life—at my job. I need to feel that my life is making a difference—that my time, knowledge, and skills are valued, and that I am respected for what I contribute to the whole. If I do, I am happy. If not,

I'll be looking for somewhere else to spend most of my waking hours.

A company is people—not brick and mortar, not products or websites, not even dollars and cents. To have a great company, you need to have—and keep—great people. In a positive workplace, people encourage each other to raise the bar. They look for ways to improve themselves and inspire each other to greatness. When the inevitable problems come up, positive people look for solutions; they don't complain and point fingers.

No matter where they reside on the organizational chart, all employees deserve the same measure of respect. The courtesy of saying "please" and "thank you" that we are taught as children is too often forgotten in the business world. Yet those simple words hold real meaning and go a long way toward making people feel appreciated for their efforts, particularly when they're called upon to do something out of the ordinary or at the last minute.

A positive culture in the workplace also allows for staff to flex their schedules when needed. At Farran Media, we want staff to achieve balance between their professional and personal lives. We allow employees to take time out for volunteer causes that are near and dear to them, to work from home occasionally, and even to bring their children to the office under special circumstances. A visit from an employee's dog lends a welcome break from the normal routine and gives everyone a glimpse of a co-worker's life outside the office.

When a company founds its culture on the Golden Rule—treat others as you would want to be treated—its employees know they will be heard, valued, trusted and treated with respect. The company becomes a community where everyone contributes a vital role to the success of the whole.

TRUST YOUR EMPLOYEES TO DO THEIR JOBS

*You may be deceived if you trust too
much, but you will live in torment
if you don't trust enough.*

—*Frank Crane*

I can't do it all. No one can run a business alone. Start it up, maybe, but run it? No way. Small businesses average about five employees. But if you want to grow that company to fifty employees and beyond, you have to hire people you can trust, love, and respect, because you'll have to delegate.

Trust is hard, especially for those of us who like to have our hands in many pies at once. I love knowing what is going on in all my departments. But I've learned that micromanaging rarely yields positive results. It shows your employees you don't trust them, don't value their work, or don't believe they are capable of completing a task on their own. You can't give someone the responsibility for something without giving her the authority to make it happen.

Here's an example: Let's say you give your employee, Greg, the responsibility for taking care of the landscape maintenance at your company, yet you require that he run every decision by you first. He's not authorized to fire the existing lawn service company if he decides it is not up to par. He's not allowed to bid out for services, and if you receive bids for three different price points, he's not allowed to pick the right company.

How is Greg going to feel? Greg is going to feel demoralized and as though he isn't accomplishing anything.

If you put someone in charge of marketing with the responsibility of getting more new customers, give that person a budget and get out of their way. They must have the authority to decide how to allocate that budget, whether on direct mail, ads on the Internet, Yellow Pages ads, social media, purchasing an email list, hiring a public relations firm—whatever they decide will be the most effective. *Delegation* translates into: "I'm giving Kerrie the responsibility for the marketing department. I'm going to give her an agreed-upon budget, and then I'm going to get completely out of her way."

Then every month and at the end of the year I'm going to meet with Kerrie and review her performance. If I told Kerrie she needed to raise our number of new customers from twenty to forty, and she came in at thirty, then it's up to me and Kerrie to figure out whether she was short money in her budget or whether she put too much advertising money toward a medium that didn't work as well.

My media company currently has a six-person sales team. I'm almost never involved in the relationships the sales team has with its clients. I'm not included in the emails (nor should I be), and I don't need to stand over their shoulders to make sure things get done. I delegate because I trust them, and I want them to know it.

This isn't to say I don't monitor. With sales, it's easy because I can just look at the revenue they're bringing in each month. Departments like editorial are a bit more difficult to monitor. Find ways to keep up-to-date about what is going on without micromanaging. Ask for updates during short, regularly scheduled production meetings. Give suggestions. Consult. But ultimately, trust your employees to do the job you hired them to do.

Trust branches out into more areas than just trusting employees to be responsible and accountable to their job tasks. It also includes trusting the way your employees manage their time. For example, when I started in dentistry, offices wouldn't allow personal phone calls during office hours. I always thought, "This is crazy!"

If you have hired independently motivated people, this should never be a problem. This is a trust issue. You don't keep a spouse faithful by keeping her locked in the closet at home. You've got to let the spouse stay faithful on her own. You've got to let go.

I know that sometimes during the day, my staff need to be emailing or texting or calling their spouses or children. Seventy-five percent of my staff members have children, after all. When I was hiring, I realized most of my office staff consisted of moms. If someone is calling from the elementary school because little Johnny has a fever, or a husband calls because he can't remember which kid to drop off where and when, that's important. I wouldn't feel comfortable ignoring a phone call from any of my four sons, so why should I expect other moms, dads, and spouses to do so?

It goes back to treating others the way you want to be treated.

I trust their accountability. If something needs to be done by a certain deadline, it will get done. And if you've got a quality employee, the ten minutes of personal time they spent on the phone trying to figure out family logistics are not going to affect this deadline or the quality of work they put in to make the deadline. If you have dedicated staff, they're going to get it done—even if it means taking some work home or working on a Sunday afternoon.

Too many people in the business world refuse to delegate; they insist upon controlling every single aspect of the business. That's why so many of them are stressed out. They don't delegate because they don't fully trust their employees. Why is that?

As a dentist, you want your patients to trust you. That's why you went to school for up to twelve years and have credentials hanging on your wall. That's why you dress professionally. That's why you're a member of the American Dental Association and why you take hundreds of hours of continuing education each year. I've given more than a thousand lectures in dozens of countries. For more than twenty years, I've asked dentists in the room if they brought their staff with them. The docs who bring their employees with them usually bring in more than $1 million annually; the docs who don't are burned out, give out negative vibes, often are struggling to keep their practices open and usually do less than $500,000 a year.

These docs don't bring staff to these meetings because they don't trust them. Why is that? They don't want them to hear what's wrong with the practice? Fine, but I bet the staff knows what the problem is already; the doc doesn't trust them!

The docs who bring their teams to lectures laugh out loud when

I talk about problems in the office. I've seen dental assistants in the crowd wad up a piece of paper and toss it at the doc's head in jest when I mention something specific that doc is doing wrong. They all trust each other. Nobody's perfect. Everyone makes mistakes. These teams understand that.

In the unhealthy office, the dentist says to her staff, "I am going to buy an in-office computer aided design/computer aided milling [CAD/CAM] machine" (which, for your understanding, dear reader, is this really cool machine that makes crowns in an hour right in your dental office—kind of like LensCrafters for teeth). The assistant doesn't say a word, because arguing is either pointless or could get her reprimanded or fired. The assistant might think it's the worst idea in the world, but she knows the doctor doesn't value her opinion, so she won't provide feedback.

After I've taken an impression of a tooth, I give it to my assistant Jan to give to the lab to make a crown or a denture. Either I'll never see it again or Jan will come back and tell me that it needs to be redone. She would know if I took a lousy impression because she knows what the lab will and will not accept. Because I trust Jan and my lab, I'll retake the impression. I never argue. If it's not good enough for Jan, it's not going to be good enough for my lab, let alone my patient's mouth.

I can't count the number of dental assistants I've encountered at seminars who tell me they, and their labs, don't dare question the dentist's work because they risk getting fired.

After I got out of dental school, the owner of the Ahwatukee dental lab, Elizabeth "Lizzie" Curran, often invited me to come spend the day with her in her lab. I would agree and pay her a visit. I only saw my own impressions that went off to her lab, but every day the lab received hundreds of impressions from scores of other dental offices. Lizzie took the time to go through all these impressions with me, to tell me what was right and wrong with each one of them. I stayed humble (another one of my core values). I knew what I knew, but I didn't know what I didn't know. By being humble and trusting, I allowed Lizzie to make me a much better dentist. (Lizzie is now an assistant professor and director of dental laboratory technology at A.T. Still University's Arizona School of Dentistry & Oral Health and is considered the patron saint of dental laboratories.)

Whenever I took continuing education courses, I'd invite my staff to go with me. Jan always looked over the course offerings at each convention and pointed me to the ones focused on areas in which I needed to learn more. She would go to the courses with me, which made implementing any new technique so much easier because she kept a list of all of the products we were going to need. She also networked with dental assistants who worked with older, experienced dentists and would take home as much knowledge from them as we gained from the seminar itself.

It all started with trust.

RESPECT YOUR EMPLOYEES AND WHAT THEY BRING TO YOUR BUSINESS

Establishing a mutual respect between employees and a boss is a delicate balance.

If you respect your employees and treat them like it, they will return the respect.

So how do you show respect to your staff? First of all, ask your employees for ideas and input. If a staff member comes up with a new idea to improve your business, she often will have no problem in helping to implement it. It is so important to create a sense of ownership among your staff. They are part of the business, which means they are also part of the business's success. Make them feel like it!

For example, if you have $10,000 at the end of the year and are trying to decide whether to remodel a portion of your office or invest the money into your marketing budget, ask your staff. They will likely have all sorts of insights. They see parts of the business you don't. They've had conversations with customers that you haven't. They may have a totally different viewpoint to bring to the table. So why not utilize their experience?

Asking for input helps staff feel involved rather than undermined. As a dentist, it's very important how products and instruments work and feel in my hands. I personally like a specific type of glove, but when I asked my hygiene staff about the product, I learned they didn't like it at all. Because I asked for their input, we ordered a different product. Everyone wins because my staff is happy. They feel involved in the decision-making.

In a 2009 article published in *Forbes Magazine*, authors Ken Blanchard and Terry Waghorn write:

> It isn't complicated. When leaders treat their people as their business partners and involve them in making important decisions, those people feel respected, and respect leads to trust. If you respect your people and they trust you as a leader, they will give their all to get the best results they can for your organization.

And frankly, it's that simple.

Respect doesn't *just* mean respecting them as people, but also respecting their time and the quality of their work. The line between work and home gets blurry. To promote the balance between personal life and professional life, you can't devise a structure that dictates the daylight hours from eight to five are all work and no family, and evening hours from five to ten are all family with no work. Those are old concepts that come from the industrial revolution and working on an assembly line. They don't apply now. It's so important for bosses and employees to have a balance between family life, professional careers, health, and spirituality. If employees feel a mutual respect, these blurred lines won't be an issue for anyone.

My company president, Lorie, is the type of person who will wake up at six in the morning and reply to emails even though she hasn't showered yet and won't be at the office until eight. She enjoys work and is a problem solver. She goes above and beyond. Obviously Lorie is an extreme example, as I don't expect any employee to get up at six and start work, but this is how she reciprocates the trust and respect I give her at the office. I appreciate this about her and I often tell her so!

We have thousands of textbooks filled with business concepts, but trust and respect are the ones I both live and swear by.

Think about your personal dealings with companies that have failed you in the past. Do you ever revisit a company you don't trust? Do you ever consider patronizing a business you don't respect? Really give this some thought. The businesses you don't trust or respect are the ones you don't give a second thought to. If you don't trust or respect them, it's likely their teams aren't managed with those values in mind either.

When you honor your employees with your utmost trust and respect, they not only give it back to you, they give it to your customers. Nobody wants to let down someone they respect. Nobody wants to lose the trust of someone they respect. So they will do their best to keep that trust at all costs. And how do they do that? By ensuring your customers trust and respect *them*! When you trust and respect your employees, everyone wins.

ACTION POINTS

- Do you trust your employees enough to delegate responsibility to them? If not, why? Do you need new people or a new attitude?
- Don't micromanage; it only shows a lack of trust. You can't give someone the responsibility of a task without the authority to get it done.
- Trust your employees enough to give them opportunities for learning.

- Respect the opinions of your employees, just as you do your customers'.
- Respect the way your employees balance their work life and personal life.

Trust takes years to build, seconds to break,
and forever to repair.

—Anonymous

Know Your Customers

*There is only one boss. The customer.
And he can fire everybody in the company
from the chairman on down, simply by
spending his money somewhere else.*

—Sam Walton

According to its 2010 annual report, Costco, the largest membership warehouse club chain in America, had 58 million members worldwide. How can it boast so many members? Costco focuses on its target audience—bargain hunters—and exists for them. There aren't any frills in a Costco warehouse. Everything is stacked on pallets. It keeps its overhead low so it can offer its customers the lowest price possible. In fact, if Costco's management thinks the price of a product is too high, they won't stock it.

Look at McDonald's. This fast food chain serves millions of people each day. That's quite a feat. But how did it get there? It focused on its target audience: people looking for fast food, consistently delivered at a low price.

Costco and McDonald's are perfect examples of massive billion-dollar businesses that have identified their customers and provide the best service they could to these customers. But how do YOU figure out who your customer is? You begin with demographics. Who are you trying to serve?

- Is this person male or female?
- How much money does this person make a year?
- Do they drive new or used cars?
- Do they eat dinner out often, and if so, at what kind of restaurant?
- How old is the person you're going after?
- What sort of education does this person have?

If you don't know the answer to any of these questions, your next step is to actually find out. How? By asking questions and paying attention. Who's showing up? Who is most interested in your product/service? What purpose are you serving? Do they want low cost or are they willing to pay a premium? Remember, you cannot dogmatically force feed the market. They either want your product at your price or they don't.

Every successful business has an obvious client base, whether your vertical is in food, transportation, utilities, or health care. Dentistry has an obvious client base made up of people who want to keep up their oral health, improve their smiles, or get relief from tooth pain—whether they want a root canal and crown, or the low cost option of extracting the tooth.

My first demographic decision had to do with the average median household income. If I wanted to focus on root canals, crowns, bleaching and tooth-colored fillings, I needed to target the upper half of the median household income. If I were going to focus on low-cost silver fillings, extractions, and dentures, I would focus on the lower half of the median household income. I chose to sell high-priced dentistry instead of low-priced dentistry, focusing on the upper half of median household incomes in my area of Ahwatukee, Arizona, where the median household income is around $80,000.

Once I knew the price I was targeting, I asked myself, "Who makes most appointments?" My team and I found that mothers make more than 80 percent of dental appointments. They not only make appointments for their children and themselves, they also typically make the appointments for their husbands.

So, we targeted all of our marketing efforts to Mom. We ran ads in the local newspaper that targeted Mom. We placed ads on shopping carts at the local grocery store. We sent out direct mail pieces focusing on Mom, meaning we promoted tooth-colored fillings in a kid-friendly environment.

Merry-go-round at Today's Dental (idea borrowed from Ray Kroc, founder of McDonald's)

As I mentioned, my practice is located in a busy plaza frequented by families, in contrast to the traditional dental office buried in some medical building off the main street where no one knows it exists.

Knowing that we're target marketing to Mom, we also parked a nice, colorful merry-go-round in front of the practice, so Mom knows instantly that our practice is kid friendly.

Today's Dental area for children (idea borrowed from Ray Kroc, founder of McDonald's)

And when Mom and the kids walk through the door, they're greeted with a bulletin board featuring the "No Cavity Club" right next to a playroom in the waiting area, similar to the play areas in many McDonald's restaurants.

DEFINE YOUR MARKET—PICK TWO

As I have said, you can't be all things to all people, especially in business. You simply cannot have the highest quality, the best service, and the lowest price; it is simply impossible! As a small business owner, you can only focus on two of these three features. You have to determine who you are and what makes you unique. You have to determine which customer segment you want to serve.

Consider McDonald's. I know you have eaten at McDonald's. Why do you eat at McDonald's? For health reasons? Probably not. You eat there because you get great *service* (e.g. a hamburger in under five minutes) at a really great *price*! What if McDonald's introduced a twenty-dollar hamburger and tried really hard to add *quality* to its mix? It would fail in a minute! McDonald's is a multi-billion-dollar business because it focuses on two things: convenient *service* and low *prices*. If you are running a McDonald's, your customers are not looking for a filet mignon. No one takes their prom date to McDonald's— that's not the market they're trying to serve.

Let's look at Costco or Sam's Club. They sell the highest *quality* name-brand products at the lowest *price*. The floors are concrete, the stuff is stacked twenty feet high. The place looks like a warehouse (because it *is* a warehouse), and the checkout lines are long. Do you think that's good *service*? Of course not. Costco and Sam's Club are billion-dollar companies because they focus on two things: *price* and *quality*. The customers at Sam's Club don't need to be pampered.

Now, how about BMW? What does BMW focus on? You guessed it: *quality* and *service*. BMW wants to make a car so great with the best customer *service* available that it forgoes price. BMW knows a certain segment of the market doesn't care about *price*; they want to buy an awesome car so they can feel hot, cool, and sexy. It's an emotional purchase.

You can't be everything to everyone.

PRICE

Price is key. Some of the biggest companies in the world—Southwest Airlines, Wal-Mart, IKEA, and Home Depot—are extremely focused on price. Where I live, one of the local grocery chains, Bashas', tries its hardest to compete on price, but any time a Wal-Mart moves in close to a Bashas' store, the Bashas' ends up closing its doors. They can't compete with Wal-Mart's incredibly low prices.

According to a UCLA study, price is the number-one deciding factor for males in choosing a new dentist, and more than 33 percent of new patients overall choose their dentist based on price. Dentists who focus on this element need to position their prices the right way in order to attract more customers.

If you focus on price, you need a keen understanding of what your competitors are doing and how they're pricing for similar goods and services. For example, dentists need to understand that if they offer both silver fillings and tooth-colored fillings, they're competing on price and giving their customers an option, rather than giving them only one choice. The more choice you can offer your customers, the better you can compete on price.

At Meineke—a successful nationwide chain of car care centers—you're always the driver. You choose one of three price points: Basic, which means "just fix it" at the lowest price; Preferred, meaning make it like new and include higher levels of inspection and parts with extended warranty; and Supreme, the most complete service Meineke offers, including parts with extended warranty and performance enhancements.

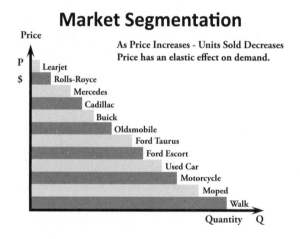

Market Segmentation

If you're in the business of selling cars, you must first determine which market segment you're going after: high-priced Cadillac or Toyota Lexus, or low-priced Chevrolet or Toyota Corolla.

Most businesses simply produce a product and then arrive at a price by adding profit, because they need a profit and figure they deserve one.

That process is completely backwards. They're specifically targeting no one, and they're going to get their lunch eaten by someone who is laser-focused on that price segment. That's what's known as market segmentation.

QUALITY

So what is *quality*? What does *quality* mean to you? Most business-people equate quality with high-priced luxury products: Rolls-Royce equals high quality; Hyundai equals low quality.

This is just flat-out wrong.

If I ask one hundred dentists where they rank in *quality*, ninety will say they are in the top 10 percent. That's mathematically impossible.

When it comes to dentistry, our patients do not even know or understand *quality*. I don't know of a single dentist who ever finished a root canal and had the patient ask to see the final periapical X-ray. I've been in practice for more than twenty-five years and it has never happened to me. I've never heard a patient ask, "Aren't you a little short of the apex?" or, "Are you sure there wasn't a fourth canal?" or, "Did you miss the MB2?"

Patients mostly concern themselves about whether or not the procedure will hurt, if the office accepts their insurance, the office hours are convenient, the staff is friendly and helpful—things like that. Yet when asked why they think you are high *quality*, patients often mention technology-related features such as intraoral cameras, paperless offices, digital X-ray images the patients can take home, or the ability to make a crown in the office in one appointment. More than 18 percent of new patients pick their dentist based on technology, according to a UCLA Anderson New Patient Study conducted and paid for by New Patients, Inc.

Do your customers buy from you because you offer the highest quality product? If so, you have to keep delivering it. If not, you have to determine the level of quality your customers expect from you. A high-tech office is a surefire way to position your practice as high-tech in the mind of your consumer. Perception = Reality.

Whether you focus on price, quality, or service, consistency is key. Consistency means you say you will give your customer X and you provide exactly X, when and how they want it—and that you do it consistently.

Quality can equal *consistency*.

So What is Consistency?

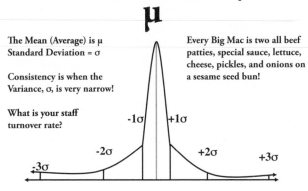

The Mean (Average) is μ
Standard Deviation = σ

Consistency is when the Variance, σ, is very narrow!

What is your staff turnover rate?

Every Big Mac is two all beef patties, special sauce, lettuce, cheese, pickles, and onions on a sesame seed bun!

Every Big Mac consists of two all beef patties, special sauce, cheese, lettuce, pickles, and onions, on a sesame seed bun. You can step into any McDonald's anywhere around the world and if they offer a Big Mac, you know what you're getting. You don't even have to worry about it. From Alaska to Australia, a Big Mac is a Big Mac—it always tastes the same. Consistency is key. McDonald's is incredibly consistent.

Low Consistency is When You Have a Large Variance!

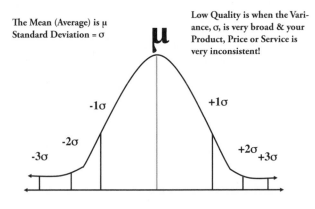

The Mean (Average) is μ
Standard Deviation = σ

Low Quality is when the Variance, σ, is very broad & your Product, Price or Service is very inconsistent!

Now, poor consistency is when you have a large variance in your product or service. A large variance means a big distribution. This is when your product, your price, or your service is very inconsistent. Let's say you go to McDonald's and the Big Mac only has one patty, and then the next time you go there it has two patties and no cheese. The next time you go it has three patties and it's twice the price as it was the week before. Frustrating, right?

My point? Tighten your variances and improve your consistency, *especially* when you're talking about price, quality, and service.

Any consultant in dentistry will tell you that the number-one perception of quality in the eyes of your patients has virtually nothing to do with your dentistry but everything to do with your staff. When patients come in for a cleaning, they expect consistency. They expect the same hygienist to clean their teeth.

In a service business, the most important indicator of quality is the consistency of your staff. When your customers come in and there is someone different behind the register every time, it throws up a red flag to the consumer that something is wrong. The employee turnover formula is one of the biggest predictors of success in a dental office or any other high-end, quality service industry where customer relations are paramount (especially when it comes to sales). According to the United States Bureau of Labor Statistics (BLS) there are about 300 million Americans and about 136 million jobs (as of May 2013). The previous year the BLS cited 4.6 as the median number of years that wage and salary workers had been with their current employer.

Employee Turnover Formula

$$\frac{\text{Time}_1 - \text{Time}_2}{\text{Time}_1} \times 100\%$$

$$\frac{50 - 30}{50} = \frac{20}{50} = 0.4 \text{ or } 40\%$$

Among dentists who make average production and average net income, I see a similar staff turnover rate. But whenever I visit the big boys and girls—the dentists grossing more than $1 million, taking home $200,000 to $400,000 a year—it is nothing to find three or four employees who have been with the doctor ten to twenty years. Reducing employee turnover is how you deliver consistent high quality and build relationships with your clientele.

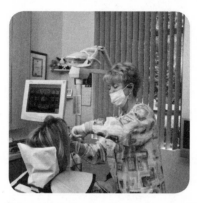

My first employee, Jan, is still with me, since 1988.

Since 1988, any patient who calls my office will speak either to me or to my assistant, Jan, who has been a member of my team from day one. My patients trust me in large part because a great person like Jan has stood beside me for more than a quarter of a century.

Consistency builds trust. You have to build *trust* with your customers, and you can't do that with a revolving-door staff.

This is why your business success begins with people. Your people are the most important part of your business. People are everything.

The only way to deliver consistent service is to have the best people you can find stay on your team for years. It doesn't matter what business you are in.

The first law of customer service is:

$$\text{Satisfaction} = \text{Perception} - \text{Expectations}$$

The First Law of Customer Service is:

Satisfaction = Perceptions − Expectations

The Second Law of Customer Service is:

It's hard to play catch up ball
once you are behind!

Arizona State University, OPM 502, Professor M. Rungtusanatham

What your customers expect is what they experienced the last time they patronized your business. The way to raise customer satisfaction is to stop employee turnover and maintain consistency. If your customers expect a great product or service and get it from you every time, they won't want to go anywhere else.

The best salesperson in any company is usually the one who has been there the longest. The new girl takes years to get up to speed, because not only is she still learning the products she's selling, she doesn't have the long-term relationships. Your long-term relationships will overcome any urge your customers have to leave you for some Groupon deal offered by a competitor.

Groupon is today's high-tech race to the bottom. Businesses that sacrifice profit just to get the sale build no customer loyalty, because the next guy that offers the same product or service for a penny cheaper is going to take that customer away.

The sooner you can tighten up your staff variance, the sooner you're going to see more long-term customers who refer their friends and loved ones.

SERVICE

Service means just that: how you and your staff serve your clients. How well your staff delivers your product or service on a consistent basis is the measure of service.

Do you have a million-dollar staff? Does your staff dive for the ball? Does your staff play to win? Do they love to talk to the customer?

In my dental practice, Today's Dental, the front office desk has a low counter with two different places to pull up a chair and sit down so my employees can talk to our patients. I cringe when I think of all the dental offices I have seen where patients are greeted by a sliding glass window that separates them from the receptionist. I find such a set-up uninviting and rude!

At Today's Dental I employ two team members fluent in Spanish, as more than 25 percent of the people who live within a five-mile radius of our office speak Spanish. This is a great service!

There are noticeable differences in service wherever you go within any industry. Let's take getting your oil changed for example. Let's say you take your car in for an oil change at one of those low-cost, quick lube places. You're greeted by the service tech and asked to have a seat in a no-frills waiting area. They change out your oil for a low price and try to upsell you on other items and services they offer.

On the other hand, when you take your car to a Lexus dealer, you're greeted by a concierge who takes your keys and ushers you to an area where you can drink gourmet coffee with a high-quality snack—all for free. You sit in a leather chair in front of a big-screen TV. The magazines are new, as is the newspaper. They offer Wi-Fi if you want to work on your laptop. And just when you're ready to take a nap, the concierge comes to take you to your car. They changed your oil and, by the way, they also washed your car and vacuumed the inside, as a courtesy.

Big difference in service offerings, especially when you go to pay the bill.

Once you have decided which two of the three—quality, price, or service—your business offers, now you have to communicate those features to your customers—whether face to face in the office as internal marketing, or via external marketing, such as your website, e-newsletters, and social media such as Facebook and Twitter.

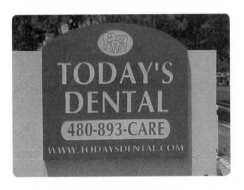

My signage, the children's merry-go-round out front, and my waiting room with its bulletin board and play area, are physical forms of marketing. We also use social media forms such as Facebook.

Today you hear a lot of hype about social media—Facebook, Twitter, Pinterest—for marketing your business. However, trust accounts for what attracts 80 percent of new customers. We especially capitalize on our social reputation, on word of mouth. We try to encourage positive online reviews. When we have a happy patient, smiling from ear to ear, we give them a list of eighteen online review sites and ask that they take a minute to log onto one and tell folks we did a good job. If you don't ask, you don't get.

Top 18 Review Sites

- Google
- Ask
- CityVoter
- Citysearch
- iBegin
- Bing
- Dogpile
- NoMoreClipboard
- Yelp
- Wellness
- Yahoo
- Demandforce
- Superpages
- MojoPages
- Manta
- Local
- Yellowpages
- Lycos

We also ask patients to refer friends and family to our office, and we send a gift to every patient who does. Maybe it's a coffee mug filled with peanuts, sugarless chewing gum, or free movie tickets—something unexpected.

Our name is also our website, which makes it easy for people to remember. You need a compelling website if you want to compete. Your website is as important in the virtual world as your location in the physical world.

Mobile Web

Mobile browsing is slated to surpass desktop browsing in **2014**.

Your website must also be mobile friendly.

Search Engine Optimization

75 percent of search engine users never go beyond the first page.

When it comes to marketing, you need to find a search engine optimization (SEO) expert. I'm in Phoenix, Arizona, the fifth largest city in the United States with 3.4 million people. When you go searching for a dentist in my area on Google, I'm listed #1, #4 and #5 on the first page of the search. That kind of placement is to die for. There are 117 towns with more than 100,000 people in America and SEO is extremely important in those markets, so find someone good to help you out. If you're in one of the 19,033 towns with populations under 100,000, SEO gets a lot easier. We chose our suburb *Ahwatukee* as the main search term, as opposed to *Phoenix*, which would encompass consumers 30 miles away.

A team with a great attitude is the best marketing of all!!!

The best marketing of all is a team with a great attitude!

TREAT YOUR CUSTOMERS WELL

Once you have identified your customers, the real work begins. How can you make sure that they remain your customers? No matter what your business, the way you must deal with customers remains the same.

Given the choice between competence and kindness, most people will tell you they'd prefer to hire a professional who is competent over kind. But why can't competence and kindness go hand in hand? Southwest Airlines hires on attitude and trains for skill.

"Chair-side manner" is not exclusive to dentists or physicians. Although you might not think this is important, clients do. In fact, to some, it's just as important as the treatment, product, or service you are selling them. If it wasn't so important, there wouldn't be a gazillion books and consultants in every industry out there helping everyone do a better job of it.

In my office, we ask each new client questions similar to those we ask any prospective employee:

- Why did you leave your last dentist?
- What did you like best about your last dentist/dental office?
- What did you like the least?
- What would you change about your last dentist/dental office?
- What wouldn't you change?

Here are some key rules to developing strong customer relationships:

Demonstrate empathy and sympathy. Empathy is the ability to mutually experience how your customer feels. Sympathy is caring about and understanding their suffering. In dentistry, we have to remember we're doing things that cause pain and discomfort for people. No one *likes* getting a root canal. We need to remind our desensitized selves that the person in the chair is often uneasy and afraid.

Every industry has the same issues. No one wants a flat tire, a computer crash, or a flooded basement. You have to put yourself in your customers' shoes. Read their cues. Let them know you're on their side. Empathize with them as you've been in their shoes and sympathize that you understand what they're experiencing.

Always give it to them straight. No matter what business you are in, tell it like it is. I'll tell a patient, "I don't take your insurance," or, "I do take your insurance"—whichever is true. I'll say, "I'm sorry, I can't save this tooth, it's got to come out," or "Fortunately I can save this tooth, but unfortunately it's going to cost $2,000 for a root canal and a crown."

Harvard Study: Adult Learning

Verbal

100 percent of what the speaker wanted to say was said...
80 percent was said
60 percent was heard
40 percent was remembered after three hours
15 percent was remembered after three days
0-5 percent was remembered after three months

Average Dental Practice Consult

Verbal + Visual

60% after three days
40-50% after three months

Top 1% Dental Practice Consult

Verbal + Visual + Notes

80% after three days
60-70% after three months

A study conducted at Harvard University showed that people are significantly more likely to remember communication that is both verbal and visual than they are to remember verbal communication alone. For example, if I give a patient an image of his broken tooth on an 8 × 10 piece of paper, circle the cavity, and write down notes and the price of the root canal, she's going to better understand and be more able to make decisions about her treatment.

Some auto insurance companies literally email you photos of your car as it's getting repaired. They show you the damaged bumper, they show you the new bumper, and they explain everything that's going on in plain English. Look into your customer's eyes when you speak, explain so he or she can understand your words, use visuals, and be sure to pull out a pen or pencil and make easy-to-understand notes so they have a better chance of remembering several months later.

Prepare your customers. If you give customers the details and let them in on exactly what you're doing, they'll appreciate you more.

And you have to speak in plain English (providing they speak English). Dentists shouldn't spout off a mouthful of dental school jargon that only they understand. If I'm going to you as my CPA, I don't want to hear accounting lingo (except, perhaps, for "refund"). When I get my oil changed, don't bother asking me whether I want thirty-weight or forty-weight oil. I have no idea what that means. Explain why I'm doing right by accepting your advice.

Talk to your clients in a way they understand.

Listen. Your customer's body language tells a lot. Be sure it doesn't say, "I can't wait for this to be over," or, "I'd rather just get this done than listen to you." Give clients your full attention. They are your number-one priority while you are at work. The customer you are working with is the only person who matters at that moment. You have to block out all other distractions. Customers who feel ignored will always find somewhere else to go, I promise you.

Never interrupt and don't think about what you're going to say next until after you've listened to them. Even if you disagree with them, be polite. Make eye contact. Reiterate their concerns. Today, more than ever, people are so distracted. It is difficult to have a discussion when you're checking your phone every five seconds. Focus! Turn it off! Spend more time with your customers pressing the flesh. Every successful millionaire is always "running for mayor." They're always asking helpful questions. "How does that tooth we fixed feel?" "Did you like Andy, the serviceman I sent out to your house?" "Is there anything else you need?"

Adapt. For me, when someone sits down in the dental chair, I can gauge fairly quickly if they're nervous or relaxed. If they're nervous I might ask if they want nitrous oxide. If they're calm, they may just want to know I'm competent, so I'll ask if they have any questions. I need to be able to read each client and accommodate their needs. Learn to recognize what clients want from you and adapt your style to deliver it. Some people buy on data and information, others buy on the emotional relationship and trust. Does your customer need more data or do they require more reassurance?

Show clients you care. In all businesses, not only in dentistry, "chairside manner" extends far beyond the point where the customer leaves your office. In the evenings after I perform an invasive procedure on a patient, my office makes "we care" calls. We ask the patients how they're feeling and if they have any questions. Sometimes these calls catch patients off guard, but in a good way. Follow up with your clients. Make yourself available to answer any questions they might have. Show them you care even after you've collected their money.

After each one of my four babies were born, the same obstetrician came by their mother's hospital room to visit and hand her a single-stem rose, just to see if she was okay. The gesture made her cry each time.

Every time I bring my Lexus home from the dealership, they always call me the next day to ask, "How was everything?" Quite frankly, I love it because at least half the time, I have a question.

Harvey Mackay—bestselling author of *Swim with the Sharks (Without Being Eaten Alive)* and *Beware the Naked Man Who Offers You His Shirt*, one of my business idols, and among the guest lecturers during my MBA program at Arizona State University—taught his sales force to fill out answers to sixty-six questions regarding every single customer.

Mackay realizes that humans are relationship-based. It starts with their families, church, and community. People are very tribal. That's why they like the local sports teams. As you know more and more and more about your customer—where they went to college, their favorite sports teams, how many kids they have and what their names are—the more connected to them you become.

Make more calls! Call up that customer who roots for the same football game you do and ask what they thought of last night's big win. Next thing you know, you're on the phone with your customer, Jim, having a blast talking about the 49ers. You're socializing passionately about the game—talking about all the plays, the ups, the downs and the turmoil—while you and that customer are bonding for life.

Make more calls! Make them as you're stuck in a layover. Make them before you leave the office for lunch. Make one last call before you leave the office for the day. Commit to making one more call every single day.

Follow up with your clients. Most millionaires make a religion out of availability to everyone.

When I was in high school, my best friend, Jim Bell, and I wanted to meet the man everyone in Wichita, Kansas, talked about—Dan Carney, the co-founder of Pizza Hut. Jim and I were so young, dumb, and naïve that one day we drove over to the offices of Pizza Hut, walked in the building and when the secretary asked, "How may I help you?" we said, "We want to meet Dan Carney."

The secretary asked what it was regarding and I said, "I just want to shake his hand." She gave me a million-dollar smile, got up, and walked straight into his office.

Next thing we know, out comes Dan Carney, this legendary, multi-millionaire with 2,800 Pizza Huts, to greet us. He literally spent an hour with Jim and me, discussing all of our stupid business ideas.

Dan and I stayed in touch for many years after that. When I had to make the complicated business decision regarding, "Should I rent or should I own?" Dan gave me brilliant dissertations on the pros and cons of renting vs. leasing. After each time I met with him or talked with him on the phone, I'd wonder, "Why in the world is Dan Carney taking my calls?" Over the years I've learned that the best business-people make themselves available all the time.

Do you have an open door policy with your staff? Unless someone is in there talking with her, Lorie, the president of my company, keeps her door open. She makes a religion of availability to all of the staff. Any of our customers can call her, and she will pick up the phone. You need to always be available to your customers, your family, and your employees, because no matter what business you're in, you're in the people business.

Our final core value prompts our team to "create opportunities to make our customers feel special." For dentists I ask, why are you taking off your gloves and mask and slinking back to your office while the local anesthetic sets in? You need to take these golden opportunities to bond with your customers, share things with them and listen to them. Engage them.

The Joy of Customer Care
Valerie Williams

The literal definition of "receptionist" is "an individual employed to be the first point of contact in an office." Receptionists typically sit at the entrance of an office and perform a variety of administrative tasks including answering phone calls, making photocopies, distributing mail, signing for packages, and general office upkeep, among others.

My definition of a receptionist, however, involves a great deal more. I like to think of myself as much more than someone who sits behind a desk, barely lifting her head and eyes above the computer to say, "sign in and have a seat." I am the person who coordinates the initial events of our patients' dental experience.

I try to create an environment that is warm, friendly, and welcoming to our "extended" family. I feel empowered to be the first person to greet the patients when they walk in the door. I want their first experience in our office to be inviting, in a clean and comfortable environment.

Patients who come to a dental office, especially new patients, have their guard up; they are somewhat apprehensive and often expect the worst. They want to be heard and acknowledged whether their concerns are financial or coming from a place of pain with their teeth.

I believe I can help alleviate a person's fears and anxieties simply by the way I greet them. I find ways to connect with each person and family—to get to know them and some of what is going on in their lives. I feel that in doing so, the patient will sense a level of trust that will carry throughout the office—a trust that can foster an ongoing relationship for years.

The biggest reward in my job is the knowledge that I am building rapport and lasting relationships, and that I am touching people's lives in a positive way. From a business perspective, patients are more receptive and accepting of treatment when they are made to feel comfortable in a friendly, non-threatening environment.

LEARN FROM YOUR CUSTOMERS

Your customers are not just the people who buy your product. They are the people who will keep you in business—by teaching you the most about your business. If you want to reach your goals, you have to listen to your customers.

The most important thing to remember when you listen to your customers is that you have to take the bitter with the sweet. Nice compliments are fine, but they don't tell you what you're doing wrong, only what you're doing right. They're just an acknowledgement that someone thinks you're doing a good job. Great. Pat yourself on the back. Feel all warm and fuzzy, and continue on. But I *want* to hear the bad stuff. I want to hear how we messed up or could have done better. Every company has room for massive improvement. It's when you get complacent and only listen to the sweet things that you start resting on your laurels and become stagnant, preparing to get run over from behind.

Listening to good news is great to reinforce what you're doing well, but successful companies, successful leaders, and successful millionaires make a religion out of listening to the bad news. They don't get defensive. They don't start telling you why what you are saying is wrong. They listen! They don't shoot the messenger. Remember, a millionaire is simply someone who solved a problem for a million people who each gave him a dollar to solve their problem. Learn to love problems!

Ronald Reagan was once asked how he defines a successful presidency. He said, "Well, when you leave, if all of the problems are different than the problems you had when you came in, you were a good president." There are always going to be problems. Whoever solves them will rise to the top. Learn to love bad news!

Take Wendy's for example. Wendy's came up through the fast food franchise ranks under the steadfast leadership of Dave Thomas, who named the franchise after his daughter. McDonald's had always been the leader in fast food, and for years Burger King held a close second place.

When Dave Thomas passed away, second-generation leaders realized they needed to get back to the drawing board. They asked thousands upon thousands of loyal patrons to give them their honest opinions about the most minute details of their service—regarding both product and overall business—right down to, "Do you like the type of lettuce we use on our hamburgers?" Wendy's listened to everything customers said—good and bad—went back to the drawing board, retooled and executed a new plan.

As of March 2012, Wendy's overtook Burger King as the number two US burger chain. It was the first time in Wendy's' forty-year history that it ever overtook Burger King. They committed to the recipe of "quality without cutting corners."

Knowing your customers inside and out is vital to keeping your company going. After all, if you're not in business for your customers, you're not in business at all.

ACTION POINTS

- Among price, quality, and service, which two make up your focus?

- Determine whether your current game plan is working. If not, what do you need to change? Maybe you sell steaks in a vegan neighborhood. Do you need to start selling salads? Are you selling sedans in an area where people want trucks?

- Sit down with your entire team and identify your customers. What do they want and need?

- Keep your customers coming in your front door. But more importantly, keep them from leaving out your back door.
- Make sure everyone on your team is honest. Integrity is everything! Make sure they are empathetic and sympathetic to your customers.
- Do your customers know what to expect?
- Are you consistent with what you deliver?
- Do you listen to everyone: your staff, customers, competitors, and colleagues?
- Do you make a religion of availability with your hours, your financial policy, and your attention?
- Do you tell and show your customers how much you appreciate and care for them?

Your most unhappy customers
are your greatest source of learning.

—Bill Gates

8

Burnout

Remember: Albert Einstein defined insanity as "doing the same thing over and over again and expecting different results." If you stick with business as usual and nothing is changing for the better, you'll burn out.

RECOGNIZE THE SIGNS OF BURNOUT

How do you know whether you or your staff is suffering from burnout? Here are some indicators. You (or they) feel

- exhausted and overwhelmed
- unappreciated
- that there are more bad days than good days
- as though action is fruitless, that nothing is ever going to change
- as though nothing you do makes any difference
- irritable at work and at home
- that life isn't worth the effort anymore

The root cause of burnout is fear of making a decision. As my father used to say, wisely, yet crudely, "Poop or get off the pot!" The risk of a wrong decision is preferable to the futility of never making any decision at all.

If your business is stagnant or, worse, going downhill, you need to first determine the source(s) of the problem and then start making some decisions. Otherwise you and/or your staff, not to mention your business, are in danger of burning out.

DETERMINE THE SOURCE OF THE PROBLEM

Is the problem with your health?

I mentioned earlier that the best decision I make every day is at five thirty in the morning when I leave my home and go to a yoga class. A healthy business begins with a healthy mind and body; if yours aren't, make the decision to do something about it.

Is the problem with your home life?

Are you carrying the stress of issues at home into your business? Is your marriage in trouble? Are you working too much to compensate for a lifestyle you can't really afford? Are your children healthy and happy?

Decide to take whatever measures necessary—seek marriage counseling, cut back on spending, pay more attention to your children—to solve the problems in your home life. It can only serve to improve your business and help keep you from burning out.

Is the problem with your work environment—with the physical space in which you spend your working hours?

There are 168 hours in a week. If you work forty of those hours, you are spending 23.8 percent, or nearly one-quarter of your life at work. So it's important to create a space you like. Too many people settle for renting some cramped, dingy office with no amenities—not even a place to put your feet up. The moment you arrive, you want to turn around and go back home. Your office sets the scene for your business and if the scene is grim, that's exactly how you and your staff will feel.

The best way to create an inspiring space is to own it.

I love coming to work every day. Know why? I own my own land. I own my own building. I share a parking lot with a grocery store and a bank. It is "Mom central" over here—perfect for a dental practice since we all know Mom makes the most appointments. I get at least one new-patient walk-in every day. My practice is visible on all sides of a busy intersection. Inside my office I have a break room, my own office space, a fridge, TV, and radio. If I need a break, I've got somewhere to go. I try to make the office as comfortable as possible for my staff, my patients, and myself. It keeps us all coming back.

Do you have the necessary "gear" to make your work compelling?
When my four boys were little, if I had put them into an empty sandbox, they would have gotten up and left. But if I threw in some pails, shovels, and a fleet of Tonka trucks, they'd stay there until they died of starvation.

I'm often approached by dentists who ask my opinion on whether to buy the newest technology—be it a laser or an iPad. I always answer by saying: "Will having it make you more excited about going to work? If just thinking about it puts a sparkle in your eye, then *absolutely!*"

The latest technology isn't always crucial for running a good business. How many of us actually need our iPads or smart phones? But if you think having an iPad is fun and it gets you excited about doing your job—if you risk getting a speeding ticket on the way to work because you're so excited to use the thing—you can't afford *not* to have one in your sandbox.

Are you assuming the responsibility of motivating everyone around you?
As I've said, you do not have to ride around on a unicycle while juggling bowling pins to inspire and motivate your staff. You need to hire internally motivated, happy people who work well with others and delegate responsibilities to them.

Is the source of the problem within your staff?

Do the people who work for you enjoy being around each other? Do you enjoy being around them?

An article I read in *Psychology Today* stated that the average two-year-old laughs three hundred times a day while the average forty-year-old laughs only three. Where did those other 297 laughs go? If a child doesn't like another child on the playground, he won't play with that kid. Yet when we grow up, we're often forced to work with people we don't get along with. If you're burned out, first look at the people you're playing with. Is anyone failing to do their job or creating dissension among their co-workers? If an employee isn't a good fit for your business, you need to make the decision to fire them and find someone who is.

Is the problem the culture you have established for your business?

If you want to retain a great staff, you need to create a culture where they are going to have fun. Period. If that is not the culture you have for your business, you had better make the decision to create one.

Each year, *Fortune* magazine publishes a list of the top one hundred best companies to work for. Google and Zappos are always near the top. Both placed in the top ten in 2012. What is so special about working for them?

Google strives to keep the "small-company feel" while continuing to grow. It rewards staff, which it calls "integral to its success," by providing compensation packages including competitive salaries, bonuses, and equity. Not only are employees compensated on a financial level, but Google also retains staff by providing a pleasant work environment. Google campuses include bikes and scooters to get around from one building to another. Break rooms are well stocked with brain food, and the company encourages many break-time activities such as foosball and volleyball.

This isn't to say you should go out and buy a ping-pong table for your office, but we can all learn from this environment. Our small businesses or practices can take smaller-scale measures to retain staff.

Every morning, our office manager stops on her way to work to pick up a veggie platter—perfect brain food! Celebrating anniversaries of each and every staff member is a must! Providing incentives and means of advancement within the company—all of these generate contagious staff morale.

In 2008, my staff and I took a tour of the headquarters of the online shoe and apparel giant Zappos in Henderson, Nevada. I strongly suggest that if you're in Las Vegas for fun or for a conference, schedule some time to take a tour of their facility.

They'll pick you up at your hotel on the Las Vegas strip and drive you to Henderson where you'll be greeted by some of the friendliest hosts you will ever meet. There's a lot of young blood pumping through the place. They'll guide you through each department where every employee will greet you with genuine enthusiasm. They take a lot of pride in what they do, but they work in an extremely relaxed atmosphere. There's not a single suit in the bunch.

Zappos has a nap room for its employees who've been burning the midnight oil and need a break. Zappos cares so much for its people that, if an employee's performance isn't cutting it, the company will pay that person to find a job that suits them.

Now, we all can't afford to be Zappos, but we can apply some of their tenets in our own businesses and make our offices a more employee-friendly place to work.

Culture starts with the owner. Even if you have only three or four employees, it still makes sense to have a break room. What every business needs is interesting perks, bonuses, flexibility, zero bureaucracy, and elimination of ridiculous rules. Companies have to be able to move fast, and they can't do so while mired in a stuffy culture with too many rules.

Excitement spills onto your staff. It makes your office a fun place to work. Pretty soon, everybody who walks in and out has this positive, awesome attitude. The enthusiasm increases word-of-mouth referrals, leads to more positive press, and decreases your desire to retire early. It affects the attitude, production, and quality of all of your services.

And it keeps you, your staff and your business from burning out.

ACTION POINTS

- Determine whether you and/or your staff already exhibit any of the common signs of burnout.

- Honestly evaluate the state of your body and health with a complete physical examination.

- Evaluate your space or environment and take steps to make it more fun, friendly, and comfortable.

- Consider if there is any new technology that would bring more excitement to your work.

- If all else fails, please get counseling.

> *Leadership is an active role; "lead" is a verb.*
> *But the leader who tries to do it all is headed for*
> *burnout, and in a powerful hurry.*
>
> *—Bill Owens*

Summary

Managing people is the most difficult part of the business equation, hands down. People are unpredictable and they come to you with a lot of history and predeterminations, whether they're on your team or they're your customers. Entire books have been written on the psychology of working with angry customers and lackluster employees. I'm here to tell you that you will never fully understand people, but you can effectively manage them with your HR process. It will be frustrating—some times more than others—but once you've developed a great team, work no longer feels like work. It's fun.

Managing people can take a lot of time at first, but once systems are in place, your company will start operating like clockwork. Whenever I get overwhelmed, disappointed, or saddened by people, I always re-read my favorite poem in the world, "Anyway," by Kent M. Keith (originally titled *The Paradoxical Commandments*), which hung on the wall of Mother Teresa's children's home in Calcutta:

The Paradoxical Commandments

People are illogical, unreasonable, and self-centered.
Love them anyway.
If you do good, people will accuse you of selfish ulterior motives.
Do good anyway.
If you are successful, you will win false friends and true enemies.
Succeed anyway.
The good you do today will be forgotten tomorrow.
Do good anyway.
Honesty and frankness make you vulnerable.
Be honest and frank anyway.
The biggest men and women with the biggest ideas can be shot down
by the smallest men and women with the smallest minds.
Think big anyway.
People favor underdogs but follow only top dogs.
Fight for a few underdogs anyway.
What you spend years building may be destroyed overnight.
Build anyway.
People really need help but may attack you if you do help them.
Help people anyway.
Give the world the best you have and you'll get kicked in the teeth.
Give the world the best you have anyway.

SECTION II

TIME

Introduction

At a restaurant one evening, the server came to our table wearing something resembling a tool belt stuffed with straws, forks, napkins, and other table supplies. Looking around, I noticed she was the only server with such a belt. When I asked her about it, she said, "Wearing this saves me twenty-five trips a day!"

This server understood something that too many business owners do not: the greatest expense in any business is time. The mistake too many business owners make is failing to see that their biggest cost is not real estate, equipment, insurance, or even employee salaries.

As a business owner, your greatest expense is time. It's a simple idea. But once you learn to focus on the second element of uncomplicated business—time—you'll find that it revolutionizes the way you and your people work.

I know too many dentists who are quick to blame insurance companies and a host of other outside factors for the problems in their businesses, when they should be looking at their own failure to use time well. They are unwilling to take a hard look in the mirror and admit, "My overhead is high because I'm slow, lazy, disorganized, and inefficient."

In the Olympics, the gold medal goes to the fastest runner, swimmer, or speed skater. Fastest means the best.

The same is true in business. Fastest means the highest quality.

Dentists know this. While an oral surgeon can pull all four wisdom teeth in thirty minutes, a general dentist will take at least an hour. The endodontist who specializes in root canals performs the procedure on a molar in an hour, while the general dentist routinely takes an hour and a half.

Who offers the highest quality?

Slow work is the result of a lack of knowledge, organization, and investment in training, equipment, and technology. It indicates you don't know what you're doing and that you are unwilling to invest the time and money in the training and technology you need to make your business thrive.

Working faster not only indicates greater knowledge and organization, it produces higher quality, higher income, and greater success.

The key is *managing your time*.

9

Time Management

If only there were more hours in a day . . .

That is the lament of anyone who doesn't have a firm hold on time management. We can't control time, only manage it.

I'll keep saying this until the day I die: *faster* is directly related to *higher quality*. If it took you an hour to complete a task today, why not shoot to accomplish the same task in less time tomorrow?

Considering that we only manage people, time, and money, time management is a major factor in your business's productivity. Managing your time and your employees' time will not only make your day easier and more efficient, but it will also provide your customers with a higher quality product or a better service experience, and your business will be more profitable.

If you are charging $100 for a product or service that takes you an hour to produce, while your competitor down the street charges $75 for that same product or service that takes them just thirty minutes to produce, you need to find out why—and fast. For the same hour of work, your competitor is getting twice as much done and making

50 percent more profit. Keep that up and, before you know it, you're out of business.

If you want to increase productivity, you need to master the keys to time management, for yourself and your staff.

MAKE LISTS

As he wrote in his *Almanac*, Benjamin Franklin, one of our country's founding fathers, began every day with the following schedule: "Rise, wash, and address Powerful Goodness; contrive day's business and take the resolution of the day; prosecute the present study; and breakfast." Each morning, he asked himself, "What good shall I do this day?"

He scheduled work from eight until Noon. The hours between Noon and two, he set aside to read, overlook his accounts and dine, before devoting the next four hours to work. From six until ten in the evening he scheduled: "Put things in their places, supper, music, or diversion, or conversation; examination of the day." He then retired for the day with his evening question, "What good have I done today?"

Next to the bracketed time frame between ten at night until five the next morning, he scheduled, "Sleep."

It may sound extreme, even funny, but I do the same and have since I was a freshman in high school. Every day when I wake up, I write a list of what I need to do that day. When I get done making that list, I circle the task that is my top priority—the one I need to begin working on at eight. Because the hours in a day are limited, like Ben Franklin, I sometimes block out eight hours on my calendar to remind myself to get enough sleep.

I also block out time to exercise, call my sons, spend time with my babe, etc. At night I think about what would make tomorrow a great day. Then just before I close my eyes, I ask myself, "What is the most important thing I need to do tomorrow?"

I also insist that each member of my team makes lists. I have my staff write a personal priority list outlining everything they need to do, circle the most important tasks, and prioritize them as first, second and third. The lists prepare them for the upcoming day, keep them focused, and make them more efficient and productive.

For my dental media company, the editorial staff needs to be aware of the next issue's top stories. I instruct the sales team, who are constantly on the lookout for new advertisers, to go after the whales first thing in the morning, big fish in the afternoon and the minnows at the end of the day. Your first sales call shouldn't be to a company that only placed a quarter-page advertisement in the magazine last year. The first call should be to a company known for buying monthly full-page ads. If you begin the day chasing down minnows, you'll run out of time to catch the whale.

DEFINE A PROCESS

In 1776, the great economist Adam Smith examined the way a factory made pins. He broke down the process of making pins in a pin factory and determined that, by dividing the labor needed for each step of the process, productivity soared. With one worker making the head and another the body, each one using different equipment, productivity was greater than if both workers carried out the full process.

You can revolutionize your own business by defining it as a process.

In my dental practice, for example, we once used the anesthetic lidocaine to numb a tooth. Back in the day, I would numb the tooth with lidocaine and then go back to my office where I wasted fifteen minutes sipping coffee and talking on the phone while I waited for the anesthetic to take effect.

A few years ago a new anesthetic, septocaine, came out that is twice as fast and effective as the traditional lidocaine. I asked my dental assistants to begin timing how long it took for the drug to take effect. As a result we are down to four minutes of wait time before a filling, potentially saving enough time in a day to see another patient.

Instead of spending those four minutes on the phone or drinking coffee, we stay and bond with the patient, enhancing our quality of service.

Dan Carney, who co-founded Pizza Hut with his brother Frank, mastered this process twenty-five years ago by developing the concept of the buffet. Traditionally Pizza Hut built a restaurant containing twenty-five tables where the average customer would wait to be seated upon entering. Once the customers were seated, the waitress took their drink orders. While the customer looked over the menu, she went to get the drinks. She then took their order and delivered it to the cooks who spent twenty to thirty minutes preparing the food. Finally the waitress served the food to the customers who ate, paid, and left. Start to finish, the entire process took about an hour.

Pizza Hut wanted to move things along faster. The price of the food remained the same, but now, while the servers were off getting the drinks, the customers were already at the buffet getting what they wanted. Then by the time the waitress came by with the drinks, the customers were eating. The average customer was done in thirty minutes instead of an hour. With the same number of tables, Pizza Hut doubled the return on their assets.

What Dan Carney and Pizza Hut did, essentially, was master the DuPont Formula from the 1920s. In the first two parts of this equation, profit margin is determined by net income divided by the dollar amount of sales, and the return on assets (ROA) by the dollar amount of sales divided by the value of assets.

The DuPont Formula:

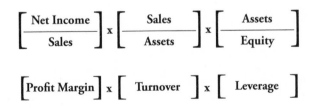

$$\left[\frac{\text{Net Income}}{\text{Sales}} \right] \times \left[\frac{\text{Sales}}{\text{Assets}} \right] \times \left[\frac{\text{Assets}}{\text{Equity}} \right]$$

$$\left[\text{Profit Margin} \right] \times \left[\text{Turnover} \right] \times \left[\text{Leverage} \right]$$

Let's say you make a profit of ten cents on a $1 sale; your profit margin is 10 percent.

Let's further assume that for each dollar in assets you have, you make one sale. (.10/1 × 1/1 = .10) Your return on assets (ROA) is 10 percent. If, on the other hand, you make two sales for each dollar in assets, your ROA will be double or 20 percent (.10/1 × 2/1 = .20).

The DuPont Formula:

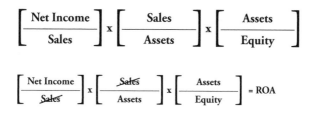

<u>R</u>eturn <u>O</u>n <u>A</u>ssets

By introducing the buffet, Dan Carney increased the number of customers he could serve at any given time, thus increasing his profit margin and his return on assets. By maximizing his use of time, he increased service to his customers as well as his income.

We'll explore the DuPont formula further in the section on money, but what is important to remember for now is the fact that efficient time management equates to higher income. It's all in the details; you start shaving off five seconds here, ten seconds there, twenty seconds here . . . Do that twenty times a day and it all adds up, allowing the same fixed asset to produce more volume.

FOLLOW THE FIVE D'S

Life comes with a host of responsibilities that might include a mortgage, car payments, household projects, and getting to little Johnny's soccer game on time—and all on top of all the responsibilities that come with running a business. The stress can pull you under.

Yet many of us make meeting our responsibilities more difficult than it has to be. I recommend you conduct your business by the Five D's—a system I learned from Lori Ross, the most successful professional dancer in the state of Arizona and a former Miss Nevada. Lori professes that following the Five D's made her number one in her field. Here are the Five D's:

1. *Design* your plan.
2. *Drop* everything that doesn't matter.
3. *Delay* everything you can't drop.
4. *Delegate* everything that can be delegated.
5. *Do* your plan.

Let's look at each of these steps more closely:

DESIGN YOUR PLAN

People who write down their goals are more successful than those who do not. What do you want to accomplish in your life before you die? Break it down by year. Then break it down by quarter. Then by month. Before you go to bed Sunday night, figure out what you want to do that week, and before you go to bed each night, decide what you want to accomplish the next day. (I love the feeling of checking off my accomplishments at the end of each day.)

DROP EVERYTHING THAT DOESN'T MATTER

If your business is failing, now is not the time to get involved in a lot of outside clubs, organizations, or leisure activities. Networking is great, but not when it interferes with attending to business. You can't improve your business while you're wasting time on emails from your buddies or checking your personal Facebook page. If you want to make money on Facebook, spend time updating your business's Facebook page. Set your priorities and focus on them.

Getting out of the gate is the most important part of a horse race. When your first decision of the day is a great, proactive decision, you have the best chance of winning the race. When your first decision is a poor, time-wasting decision, you have too much ground to make up. As Christopher McDougall writes in his book, *Born to Run: A Hidden Tribe, Superathletes, and the Greatest Race the World Has Never Seen*: "Every morning in Africa, a gazelle wakes up, it knows it must outrun the fastest lion or it will be killed. Every morning in Africa, a lion wakes up. It knows it must run faster than the slowest gazelle, or it will starve. It doesn't matter whether you're the lion or a gazelle—when the sun comes up, you'd better be running."

Drop every needless distraction and refocus on your business.

DELAY EVERYTHING YOU CAN'T DROP

Let's say you are scheduled to meet with your accountant this week to do your taxes, but you also have a deal in front of you that could make or break your business. Do you have to meet with your accountant or can it wait? Is it critical that you pick up your dry cleaning or get groceries after work, or can you meet with the new client who happens to be in town and could possibly keep your business in the black?

It's pyramid logic: you don't focus on what's at the top when your base is crumbling. Fortify your base—which includes your body and your health—and then work your way up.

DELEGATE

Why are you doing all the work? The reason Ray Kroc was so successful at McDonald's is because he spent all his time working *on* the business, not *in* the business. Throughout the 1960s and '70s, McDonald's would open a restaurant in a small town and drive the mom-and-pop restaurant out of business within thirty days. That's because Mom and Pop did everything and delegated nothing, leaving no time to work on the big picture. Ray Kroc had time to figure out how to cut the cooking time for a burger and fries from twenty minutes to three, and to discover that a majority of customers preferred the idea of a drive-through to getting out of their cars.

He worked *on* the business, not *in* the business.

If you're the business owner, you need to delegate and—as we covered in chapter 5—you need to hire the people who are going to get the job done the right way.

DO

That one word says it all. Now that you've delegated everything that can be done by someone else, you must actively engage in what is yours to do. Look at where you want to be in twenty years, what competition is coming up behind you, what technologies could revolutionize your business . . . Carry out the plan *you* designed.

CONCENTRATE ON THE THREE LEGS OF MANAGERIAL ECONOMICS

My favorite CEO remains Jack Welch of General Electric. At GE, there were more than twenty divisions that reported to Welch—divisions ranging from light bulbs and jet engines, to nuclear power plants and the National Broadcasting Company (NBC). He knew nothing about how to make a light bulb or a hit TV series, let alone how a nuclear reactor works. Rather than trying to learn everything about everything, Jack mastered the art of finding the best people. He concentrated on his team. He didn't need to know how a jet engine works; he simply had to find the best person among those who did, and then trust that person to manage the division utilizing all the most skilled employees. That's delegation, and delegation means making the best, most efficient use of your time and your employees' time.

At one point Jack Welch had 411,000 employees in different divisions spread out all over the world. Welch's management approach illustrates the three legs of managerial economics—the legs that support the purpose of any business:

1. What is the reward?
2. Who makes what decisions? (What is the job description?)
3. What is the score? (How are we going to measure our success?)

The 3 Legs of Managerial Economics

Purpose

What's the Reward?

Who Makes What Decisions?

What's the Score?

WHAT IS THE REWARD?

As we've discussed, you want your employees to feel the reward of having purpose and value in your business. In addition, you must at least pay competitive wages and salaries or your employees will find somewhere else to work.

Equity
Fair dealing with people.

• Motivate with Production Goals
• Staff must share the wealth

As for bonuses, you want to create systems that are team based, so that your employees continue to focus on all aspects of your business. I have two bonus systems: a productivity bonus for staff and management, and a more complex profitability bonus primarily for management.

Production Goal #1

Production Goal #2

Production Goal #3

For our monthly productivity bonus, we set three production goals in increments of X-number of dollars. If the staff meets the first goal, I give each employee a crisp $100 bill. If they meet the second, I give each employee two $100 bills. If they reach or exceed production goal #3, they go home with three $100 bills. I'm not offering enough money for my team to take their focus away from all the details that make my business fantastic. No one games the system for $300, but it's fun; it's a new pair of shoes and dinner out with a spouse. It works well for staff morale and encourages the best usage of their time.

Our profitability bonus is based on a more complex formula:

QCA – CI – QE = Quarterly Net Income or Quarterly Net Profit

QCA stands for Quarterly Collected Amount, CI for Capital Investment (percentage of quarterly collections that is reinvested in the business before profits are shared), and QE for Quarterly Expenses. This bonus system allows management to focus not only on what we're producing each month, but on what's being paid out of the business in overhead.

WHO MAKES WHAT DECISIONS?

This directly relates to *job descriptions*.

When I go into a business and find confusion in payables, account receivables, and collections, I always find that there are two or three different people working those areas. Since no single person is in charge, there's literally no one who holds the responsibility or authority to get anything done. In any business—large or small—every single employee must have a detailed job description. They each must have access to an organizational chart that specifies to whom they report, who directly reports to them and what decisions they are responsible for and have the authority to make. Remember: you cannot delegate responsibility to people without also giving them the authority to make decisions.

Give each one of your job descriptions the "Mack Truck Test." What do I mean? Let's say that, sadly, one of your employees gets run over by a Mack Truck. Would the next person to fill that job know what to do? Would you be able to tell them?

Were something tragic to happen to Lorie Xelowski, the president of my company who has been with me since 1998, a very smart replacement would need to know a lot of details about the job. Not only is Lorie's job description spelled out in a three-inch-thick binder, we have digital records of her emails numbering in the thousands. How to find her replacement is clearly outlined in the SOP (Standard Operating Procedures). She has even written her own recruitment ad!

WHAT IS THE SCORE?

In my dental practice, we compile data on everything. The most obvious data we track includes the number of new patients, number of patient referrals, total time for each procedure, and patient comments. The less obvious but very important data includes production versus collections, watching your receivables, and number of cancellations, to list a few. I use a different phone number for every advertisement we run—so that we can track which ads are most effective.

In a football game, there may be twenty-two players on the field, but there also are six officials, one referee, and a scoreboard keeping track of every point, so there is no confusion among the players, fans, or owners about the score. Your business, too, needs a scoreboard—one that measures every relevant piece of data that you and your team need in order to set and achieve your goals. Keep your scoreboard simple and your team focused on it every day.

A well-managed business can outlive you. Ray Kroc has been gone since 1984, yet 34,000 McDonald's restaurants open every day to bring you a burger, fries, and a Coke just the way he planned.

ACTION POINTS

- Understand that you can't control time, only manage it. Time is finite, and good time management will increase productivity.

- Get into the habit of making lists—both you and your staff. Prioritize the tasks on your list and tackle the most important tasks first.

- Define each process of your business and work to improve on each of them.

- Focus on the Five D's:

    - *Design* your plan.

    - *Drop* everything that doesn't matter.

    - *Delay* everything you can't drop.

    - *Delegate* everything that can be delegated.

    - *Do* your plan.

Lack of direction, not lack of time is the problem.
We all have 24-hour days.

—Zig Ziglar

Time must be explicitly managed, like money.
You can always change your plan, but only if
you have one. Ask yourself: Are you spending
your time on the right things? . . .
Time is all you have. And you may find one day
that you have less than you think.

—Randy Pausch (The Last Lecture)

10

Efficient Communication

The digital revolution has certainly changed the way we communicate. Back before email and cell phones, a cement truck might leave the factory only to arrive at its destination to be told the cement was no longer needed. There was no way to get in touch with the driver to tell her, "Don't go to that site; go to this one instead." Now someone just calls the truck driver on her cell phone and she takes the concrete where it's needed.

But I believe the pendulum has swung too far in the other direction. Now instead of no communication, there is too much. Businesses are over-communicating with way too many emails, texts, and meetings. Instead of increasing efficiency, they are wasting valuable time.

Communicate to save, not waste, time. After a quarter of a century in business, I've learned some measures you can take to maximize the efficiency of the communication systems in your business.

CONDUCT A MORNING HUDDLE

Begin each business day with a morning huddle.

Businesses that start with a morning huddle to discuss their goals for the day are more than twice as likely to be successful. It's all about planning. Can you imagine a football team not having a strategy meeting before the big game?

As they arrive at work, your employees' thoughts are still on their early morning routines of getting dressed, making breakfast, making sure the kids get off to school on time *with* their homework and lunch boxes.

The morning huddle is an efficient means for staff to transition from personal mode to business or "game" mode.

In our dental practice, we do what any football team does before the big game. We review our strategy and set our priorities. We define the focus for each member of the team for that day. We try to anticipate potential problems—such as an unscheduled emergency—and create solutions. Where can we work that patient into the existing schedule? Which operatory can we make available?

Similarly, if we are low on supplies, we discuss what and how to conserve until our shipment arrives.

The morning huddle is imperative for effective time management by solving problems before they happen. Clear, focused communication at the outset prevents chaos and stress throughout the day.

The Morning Huddle
Sandy Wilkinson

Our day at Today's Dental begins with a meeting we refer to as the *Morning Huddle*. We gather as a team at 6:40 a.m. and the staff in each department brings important information to share about the day.

For instance, I'll bring the financial information about

the previous day's production, the production month-to-date, and how close we are to meeting our office production goal. Assistants and hygienists bring specific patient information such as frequency of X-rays, treatment pending, patients needing pre-medication, and those with latex allergies or other medical conditions. They also discuss any patients with family members due for a recall appointment. The front office staff reports any messages from voicemail and alerts the staff to patients with existing balances. They review availability in the schedule for possible treatment of patients that day, including emergency patients.

The Morning Huddle ends with a positive quote brought by a different department each week.

Why is all of this important?

By meeting and discussing the day prior to seeing patients, we are better prepared to give our patients the best care possible as well as increase the overall flow and production of the office. An additional benefit of the morning huddle is that it forces all employees to review their schedules for the next day, helping to familiarize them with each individual patient (or customer), and perhaps find room in the schedule to perform additional procedures to better serve our patients and increase our production.

This meeting, in my opinion, is the most beneficial ten to fifteen minutes of the entire day. Being prepared lowers the stress level in the office, which, in turn, allows everyone to be more productive.

The morning huddle does not completely eliminate the need for meetings later in the day, however. Issues can and do arise that call for an impromptu discussion. If it is something that needs to be handled right away, stay focused and solve it in less than five minutes. If you determine the issue, (1) cannot be solved within five minutes, and (2) can be addressed at a later date, schedule a time to meet within the next twenty-four to forty-eight hours and then come with a specific, written agenda.

For all planned meetings, provide a copy of the agenda for everyone in attendance and strictly adhere to it. Do not allow the discussion to stray from the topic at hand and make sure everyone leaves the meeting with the same understanding of what is expected.

An effective meeting is where brainstorming occurs, ideas are born, teams are strengthened, and the mission is clarified. But stray from the agenda and you most likely will waste an hour on an issue that could have been resolved in twenty minutes. That's precious time you can't get back.

You must also develop a company dashboard. You need to post your objectives, along with the measure of how well your business is meeting those objectives, in a common area for everyone to see. Every part of every team needs to be able to see what the other teams are doing and how they fare. The purpose of giving the entire company access to all parts of the company dashboard is to provide staff with a clear view of how each department impacts the business as a whole. Often a staff member will spot potential improvements based on an entirely different department's data. For example, "I notice we're always sold out of inventory, but I also see that our overhead is too high. Why don't we consider raising our prices?"

ELIMINATE ALL NEEDLESS COMMUNICATIONS

Here are some quick and easy ways to cut down on communications clutter:

- Keep your email messages clear, concise, and focused only on the crucial points, so you aren't wasting anyone's time.
- Design your communication around your organizational chart. If you have five teams and each team has a department head, only message the person in charge. Do not waste your

staff's time by copying the message to every member of the team. Let them work and be productive.

- Don't accept unnecessary messages in your email files. Instruct your staff to copy you *only* on matters that require your decision, and allow them to unsubscribe to any emails that only waste their time.

- Take advantage of available technology such as walkie-talkies or an interoffice messaging system.

- Set up an automatic response that lets people know that you're managing your email the way you want and that if it's important, you'll get back to them ASAP. Garrett Gunderson, the author of the *New York Times* bestselling book, *Killing Sacred Cows*, created an automatic response that outlines how and when every email will be handled, and what to do if the matter is an emergency:

I rarely personally handle email; instead I use a team approach. My team will be filtering all emails. I will have meetings with them to address any items that need to be addressed. If this requires immediate attention and you know my cell phone, please text me. Otherwise someone from my team will be in touch with you. Please be assured that any attachments or items I need to see will be brought to my attention as I meet with my team on a regular basis.

In Prosperity,

Garrett B. Gunderson

P.S. This is the way I prefer to manage my time. Email can get out of control and to focus on my soul purpose this is the approach I have taken.

When I was ten and visited Disneyland for the first time, when an employee—or "cast member"—didn't know the answer to a customer's question, I saw a lot of running around while they looked for someone who did. These days they simply put the question out over their push-to-talk (PTT) microphone and everyone has an answer immediately. An all-points-bulletin can go out for a lost toddler and within seconds every staff member around the entire park is on the lookout for little Jimmy.

When I opened my practice, my receptionist spent at least a quarter of her time running around the office relaying messages. Now the entire staff is outfitted with Motorola walkie-talkie headsets, so if the receptionist gets a cancellation, she can relay it to everyone without ever leaving her desk. Everyone has all the information they need to make higher quality decisions, increase productivity and budget time more efficiently. Knowing a patient has canceled creates the opportunity to spend additional time on a patient who needs it, or to squeeze in an emergency patient.

The average company spends half of its resources on people and usually less than 5 percent on technology. Technology makes your team and your business more efficient and cost-effective.

SPEAK WELL OF YOUR COMPETITORS

During his 1966 campaign for governor of California, Ronald Reagan popularized the 11th commandment created by then California Republican Party Chairman Gaylord Parkinson: *Thou shalt not speak ill of any fellow Republican.*

In every industry, including dentistry, verbally bashing colleagues or competitors inevitably destroys your customers' trust in your profession and earns you a bad reputation. Apple didn't become a giant in the computer industry because Steve Jobs bashed Bill Gates and Microsoft. Apple kept its sights on building a superior product.

Business is a golf game, not a boxing match. You don't get to the top by tearing everyone else down. Don't worry about the competition; focus on your own game.

I fired one of my top magazine advertising salesmen because, in his presentations to clients, he always badmouthed other publications within the industry. I was so proud of our dental magazine that

I believed the entire presentation should be devoted to describing just how great a publication it is.

True story: A dentist, whom I'll call Smith, referred one of her patients who was moving across the country to another dentist, whom I'll call Jones. Months later Smith gets a surprise call from her old patient demanding to know where she went to dental school and where she got off doing shoddy work on her patients.

After calming her former patient down, Smith asked him where he got the notion that she was such a lousy practitioner. Turns out, at the patient's first visit to Jones' practice, Jones spent the entire appointment badmouthing Smith, even suggesting she should be sued.

Smith couldn't possibly try to defend herself to her patient, except to say: "I've done the best dental work I can do, and I will call your new dentist to find out why he said what he said."

So Smith picked up the phone and called Jones. She told Jones about the phone call she'd just received from her patient and asked him to tell her exactly what he thought was so "shoddy" in her work.

Jones begins talking about a failed root canal that Smith didn't even do. Smith threatened Jones with a lawsuit for slander if she ever again heard anything negative originating from Jones' practice.

You might judge a colleague as "incompetent," but frankly, you have no idea of the circumstance surrounding a report of poor performance, or whether or not it is even true. There are countless extenuating circumstances that can affect any given situation.

I don't care how competitive your local market is. If a colleague were standing in the same room, would you speak ill of her? Probably not. Then what's to be gained by bashing her behind her back?

Everyone makes mistakes. Nobody knows everything. Nothing but harm can come from sullying the reputation of your competitors—your colleagues. Give them the benefit of the doubt. And if they're in over their heads, offer them an olive branch and help them through. As I've said, a rising tide floats all boats. By supporting a colleague, you can only enhance the reputation of your entire industry and, as a result, your own business.

CONNECT WITH YOUR COLLEAGUES

Even in today's digital age—as everybody connects more frequently with Facebook, Twitter, Google+, Pinterest, and LinkedIn—professionals still attend conferences, conventions, and seminars. Why? Because, as Maslow stressed, humans are social animals who desire close, personal connections with friends, family, and peers.

You might think going to conventions is a waste of time and money—time and money better spent at your place of business. However, I can't stress enough how invaluable face-to-face meetings with your peers are to dealing with any problem you may be facing at work. Chances are that one of them found a solution to that particular problem months ago and can provide you with the answer.

Meeting with your colleagues exposes you to new ideas. It can reignite your passion and inspire you to not only work harder, but also more efficiently. Professional meetings serve as a reminder of why you got into the business in the first place.

I always tell my colleagues to take their peers, specialists, and suppliers out to lunch or dinner. I believe it is so important to maintain good relationships with those who work in the same profession all the way up and down the supply chain to gain support, business referrals and advice. The old adage is true; the whole is greater than the sum of its parts. The more people you know and network with in your industry, the greater the chance you will be successful. Whether it's breaking news on a hot new technology, the sudden availability of an exemplary worker, a special price on some major item you've been looking for, or simply the joy of sharing experiences with your friends within the industry, the benefit of networking is priceless.

I can't tell you how many times I've heard dentists questioning why they bother being members of the American Dental Association (ADA). In fact only 75 percent of dentists are members of the ADA, and less than 50 percent of all physicians are members of the American Medical Association (AMA). Often those who join only do so for the purpose of marketing themselves to potential customers—like making claim to the *Good Housekeeping* stamp of approval. These dentists might go to a convention once every few years, but that's about all the effort they're going to put into it.

Get involved! Take charge and put more into networking, because I guarantee you, the more you put into your profession, the more you'll get out of it.

It's virtually impossible to replicate an annual meeting. If you don't go, you'll miss breakout sessions, camaraderie, training sessions, motivational keynote speakers, new products, special "show-only" incentives, inspiration, and team building. You and your entire team should attend.

After my team and I attend a convention, we come back energized with at least one amazing new idea that we plan to implement immediately so that we can do dentistry faster, cheaper, with better quality, and at lower cost. As long as you have hired the right people so that your turnover is low, paying for your team to attend will yield an outstanding return on investment.

ACTION POINTS

- Start every day with a morning huddle. Use the huddle as the focal point of your office communications.
- Connect everyone with an interoffice communications system.
- Don't over-communicate via email—with your employees or your customers.
- Create a culture where it's okay to politely unsubscribe from interoffice emails.
- Always talk positively about your competition.
- Communicate with your colleagues regularly.
- Start networking more with your colleagues and up and down the supply chain.

- Invite your team to attend conventions with you.
- Next time you're on vacation, visit a colleague and invite them out for dinner.

Any tool that enhances communication has profound effects in terms of how people can learn from each other, and how they can achieve the kind of freedoms that they're interested in.

—Bill Gates

11

Learning: Time Well Spent

I n my profession, we say we "practice dentistry" because no one has perfected dentistry—and no one ever will. There's always something new to learn, whether it's a new technology or a new technique.

The same holds true for every profession on the planet. Once you've learned how to do your job or run your business, there is always something new you can learn to improve. You need to remember to take some time for yourself and, for the sake of your business, stay on the cutting edge or risk getting left in the dust by your competitors.

Don't have any time to get out of the office? Fine, go get another book from the business section of your local bookstore or Amazon.com. Remember: all leaders are readers, so keep reading! You're reading this book because you thought it might help improve things, right? Great, when you're done with this, I implore you to pick up another book that might provide more insight into how to better run your business.

As we've discussed, conventions and seminars are great places to learn. Although you might cringe at the thought of closing down the office for a day, the long-term benefits outweigh the short-term loss in revenue. I recommend you sign up for a convention or seminar right away. Why? Here's an example from my industry.

Dental associations provide dentists like me with many opportunities to broaden our knowledge and skill set. When I got out of dental school, I began taking over five hundred hours of continuing education courses per year because I wanted to learn everything at the beginning of my career. I figured the best return on investment would come at the beginning of my career, not at the end.

At the end of one particular course, I was asked, "Do you want AGD credit?" I had no idea what AGD meant. So I asked an older dentist who explained that it stood for the "Academy of General Dentistry" and insisted that I join. He told me that after completing five hundred hours of instruction and successfully passing an all-day exam, I would receive my fellowship (FAGD). Another six hundred hours and I'd receive my mastership (MAGD).

When I asked him why I should want fellowship or a mastership, he replied, "Trust me, if you follow the AGD program, you will become a better dentist." Since I knew I wanted to become a better dentist, I committed that day to earning both distinctions.

Before I joined the AGD, I only took classes in areas where I experienced issues—mostly fillings, crowns, and root canals. In order to earn my fellowship I had to take five hundred hours of continuing education courses in sixteen other segments, so I reviewed all the course options. As a young, naïve dentist just out of dental school, I thought: "Why would I want to learn about orthodontics, or placing implants, or TMJ? I don't do any of those things."

Yet my goal and commitment to earn my fellowship overruled my frustration and inconvenience, so I forced myself to learn other areas of dentistry, even though I thought I'd never use any of it in my own practice.

I remember walking in to the first day of a two-day implant dentistry course taught by Dr. Carl Misch. I felt so frustrated that I had to sit and waste two days of my life hearing about a topic I had no interest in, just to earn my fellowship.

Looking back it was as though I stumbled upon an entirely new continent. Those were the coolest two days I had ever spent in dentistry! I fell in love with Dr. Carl Misch *and* his course. The next thing I knew, I was paying for his six, two-day, hands-on surgical courses 1,500 miles away in Pittsburgh, Pennsylvania. I loved it so much I received my diplomate degree from the International Congress of Oral Implantology.

There is a reason there are 30,000 members of the AGD; they have much more successful practices than non-AGD members. It's cause and effect.

What is the AGD for your profession? Whatever it is, I urge you to join today. Consider what credentials you could commit to learning today that could positively impact your career. You will never regret the time and money you spend credentialing yourself in areas of your profession.

Joining a professional association not only broadens your knowledge base, it also broadens your network. When you're starting out in your profession, the first thing you need to realize is that you're going to make a lot of mistakes. But you'll make a lot fewer mistakes if you learn from the mistakes of other, more experienced members of your profession. Listen to their stories. Take their advice. You know what you know, but you don't know what you don't know.

LEARN FROM A MENTOR

Even if you've been out of school and in business for a long time, there is always someone doing your job faster and better than you. You need to learn from these people. The people I've met who found a good mentor at any age or step along their career all eventually ended up a success. By the time they were forty or fifty years old, they paid it forward by mentoring someone else. The best students become the best teachers.

In the four months between graduating from dental school and opening my own practice, I went to work for Ed Silker, DDS, who was the Phoenix area's most successful dentist at that time—which was the very reason I wanted to work for him. I was preparing to open my own practice, and I wanted to learn as much from Ed's experience as humanly possible.

Ed revolutionized the way dental practices operated. From the time the world's first dental school in Baltimore, Maryland, began turning out dentists in 1840, dental offices were hidden away in large medical buildings near hospitals. The first dentists to stray from the norm and open their practices in freestanding offices instead of large medical buildings were blackballed from dental societies.

Ed, my mentor, took the concept of the freestanding office to the extreme by purchasing eight prefabricated mobile buildings and dropping them onto the parking lots of shopping centers all over the Phoenix valley. The convenient offices generated hundreds of new patients at each location and his productivity skyrocketed. In my last two years of dental school, I did fifty fillings, fifteen crowns, fifteen root canals, and pulled fifty teeth. When I worked for Ed, I did the same number of procedures *every week* for sixteen weeks.

He also was among the first to advertise. Until the Supreme Court—in the 1977 landmark case of Bates vs. the Supreme Court of Arizona—found in favor of an Arizona attorney's claim that the right to advertise fell under freedom of speech, professionals in both the legal and medical fields were forbidden to advertise their services. Ed was among the first dentists in the Phoenix valley to take advantage of the opportunity and advertise in the Yellow Pages.

From Ed Silker I learned the value of both innovation and delegation. He hired an office manager for every one of his prefab offices. He gave each manager the authority to hire, fire, and run her office as she saw fit, and he stood behind every decision. As a result, his managers were happy, his turnover was low and his volume of business remained high.

I learned so much under his direction that I continued to work for him for an additional six months after I opened my own practice. I worked in my own dental office from 6:00 a.m. to 2:00 p.m. Monday through Saturday. I continued to work with him on those days from 2:00 to 10:00 p.m., and on Sundays from 6:00 a.m. to 10:00 p.m.

It was time well spent. I learned about billing, advertising—every aspect of the business.

Too many new dentists use the wrong criteria when looking for their first job. They'll consider factors such as location, how much the practice is making, and the potential of the current dentist selling the practice soon and for a reasonable price. What they should be considering is: "Can this dentist teach me how to perform quality dentistry? Can she teach me how to build a winning team? Will she teach me how to market and advertise?"

The same holds true for anyone starting out in any profession. There is so much more to think about when buying a business than a purchase price. If you have the opportunity to work for someone you admire, whether your plan is to buy a dental office or a plumbing company, I think that's fantastic. If you're a plumber shopping yourself around to get hired at one of five plumbing companies and you choose the one that pays the most money, that's so myopic! You can't base your decision on what you're going to get paid by the hour. You should care more about whether or not this person will teach you how to become successful.

That is priceless information.

LEARN FROM YOUR COMPETITORS

In my seminars, because I'm usually speaking to a room full of dentists and their teams, I'm often asked how I "deal" with the dentist from across the street. Again, I tell people to look at competition more like a golf match, not a boxing match. There are seven billion people on this planet. There will always be other restaurants, dental practices, drycleaners, plumbers, and car washes.

It's actually psychologically healthy to see what competitors are doing, but you have to realize, every business has a front door and a back door. While you're ushering in new customers through your front door, you have to keep your eye on which customers are leaving out your back door on their way to feed and grow your competitors.

The concern is not your competitors. The question is why aren't your customers coming back?

Sometimes you learn that you cannot prevail over a competitor. One of my favorite books of all time is *Only the Paranoid Survive* by Andy Grove, the founder of Intel. Andy Grove started a young business developing dynamic memory chips (DRAMs). As he was learning about his competitors and determining how to make DRAMs faster, easier, higher in quality and lower in price, he learned that he was never going to win against the Japanese. In learning from his competitors, he realized he should switch his company's focus from DRAMs to microprocessors, and the rest is history!

Sometimes in your business you might come to learn that your competitor has a cost advantage, and you're never going to win the low-cost market segment of your industry. You're competing against a company that structurally has lower costs than you. Maybe they're in a foreign country. Maybe you're in expensive, downtown New York City, and they're out in the middle of small-town rural America. You might learn from your competitors that you need to switch from producing low-cost Chevys to high-priced Mercedes.

In my dental office, the first thing I ask all my new patients (customers) is why they quit going to their last dentist. I don't want to make the same mistake the last dentist made.

If a patient of mine doesn't come back, I call to ask why. As much as I need to know why a patient leaves my competitor's office to see me, I need to know why a patient chooses to leave my office to go feed my competitor.

Business is a golf game. In golf, I spend ninety-five percent of my time working on my own game; I don't care what anyone else is doing. It's the same with my dental magazine business. I almost never read another dental magazine. Why? Because my customers email me literally a hundred times a day telling me what they want me to do for them. I have owned my magazine since 1994, and for those nineteen years I have consistently focused on meeting my customers' demands. If instead I spent my time focusing on what other dental magazines are doing and trying to be like them, I'd fall way behind on delivering what my existing customers want.

CONDUCT A SWOT ANALYSIS

I recommend doing a SWOT (Strengths, Weaknesses, Opportunities, Threat) analysis on all of your competitors. This is a perfect team exercise. I always bring in my management team and within the four squares of the SWOT analysis chart, we write down that company's strengths, weaknesses, opportunities, and threats. It's a fantastic mental exercise. It gives clarity to the team.

Let's say you're a swimmer or a cross-country runner. There's always going to be a competitor who is faster and one who is slower than you.

The same is true for your competition. It is important to analyze what they bring to the competition. What are their strengths? Do they have more knowledgeable workers? Do they offer lower prices? Do they advertise better? Do they have beneficial affiliations?

What are their weaknesses? What opportunities does their business present you?

What threats do they pose to you? Years ago I discovered there was a dentist in my community who focused entirely on the Medicare/Medicaid business and who had a much lower cost structure because he used low-cost, entry-level employees. I could not compete in the Medicare business because I employed a team of long-term employees who were highly trained and knowledgeable. So I gave up the Medicare segment of my customer base.

We made more of the middle-of-the-road Ford Taurus kind of dentistry. We knew how to be the Mercedes-Benz of dentistry, but we decided not to focus on that area because we are located in Phoenix, Arizona, not Beverly Hills. Another dentist in my area focused forty hours per week primarily on the cosmetic end of dentistry. I focused on my demographics—on providing good, solid, no frills, family dentistry to middle-class Americans.

I know of plumbing businesses in Phoenix that focus entirely on 24-hour, same-day emergency service. That's an entirely different market than plumbers who focus on residential plumbing for new construction or on rehab for older houses.

Doing a SWOT analysis of everyone competing in your market directs your focus. Remember: If you try to be all things to all people, you'll be nothing to no one and you'll eventually go out of business.

PUT IN THE TIME

In his book, *Outliers*, author Malcolm Gladwell stresses that *you have to put in the time*. Gladwell states that most successful people spend ten thousand hours before they master their success. The average person takes ten years to reach those ten thousand hours.

Consider physical fitness. There are a thousand books and just as many theories on diet and exercise, yet it all comes down to putting in the hours. If you work out every day, that's eighty percent of it.

Too often in business I see owners who want to get rich quick, to become overnight successes. They have no idea they need to put in ten thousand hours over ten years before they master anything.

The current world economy is viciously competitive and you're going to be lousy at whatever it is you're doing for your first two or three years. You'll be okay in years five through seven. But you won't be the greatest at what you do for ten, twenty, or even forty years! Business success is a marathon, not a sprint. As long as you don't give up, you'll achieve it.

Whether it is with your clients, finances, networking or new technology—you have to put in the time. Too many business owners need to turn off the television, set aside the Xbox—or any other idle distraction—and put in the time to master their business and become a success.

ACTION POINTS

- Join the association that represents your profession.
- Commit today to going to your profession's annual convention.
- Start actively looking for mentors not only in your career, but also up and down the supply chain.
- Consider becoming a mentor to someone younger or less advanced in their career than you.
- Complete a SWOT analysis on all of your competitors.
- Put in the time to master your business.

*Anyone who stops learning is old,
whether at 20 or 80. Anyone who keeps
learning stays young. The greatest thing
in life is to keep your mind young.*

—*Henry Ford*

Time with Your Clients

When my customers arrive at my dental practice, we ask for their name, insurance information, and complete health history. After that, I like to find out why they left their last dentist. I like to know what they did and did not like about their last dental practice. I get answers such as, "I loved that she was open Saturdays and that she took my insurance, but this crown she did on my front tooth doesn't match my other teeth."

Our next question is always, "What can we do to help you and what are you expecting from us today?" Remember: Satisfaction = Perception – Expectations. I want to know how we can meet or exceed this new patient's expectations.

I also want to know why, of all of the other great dentists in Phoenix, she decided to come see me. How did she find out about my practice? Was she referred? Who referred her? If Lisa referred her and Lisa is a patient of mine, I want to acknowledge and thank Lisa, whether with a phone call, flowers, or coffee mug containing a Starbucks gift card. I want to positively reinforce her action so that she knows how important it is to us. That way, she likely will refer someone else in the future.

In brief, I want to spend the time to get to know my clients.

MAXIMIZE CLIENT COMMUNICATIONS

It doesn't matter what business you're in, gather key information from every customer who walks through your door. Whenever possible, communicate with your customers face to face so that you can establish a personal relationship with them. Face-to-face communication comes easy for some; for others it is a struggle. But it is an opportunity to listen to your customers with your full attention—to learn what they need, what they want, and what concerns they have.

Phone calls to your customer also are a great form of communication. In my dental practice, we make follow-up calls to our patients after any procedure to find out how they are doing. We want our patients to trust that we continue to care about them even after we've collected their money.

The downside to phone calls is that they can be expensive and time consuming for your high-cost labor. When a personal call is unwarranted, automate your calls to make your labor more efficient.

Back in the day, my practice used to call patients to confirm their appointments; now we automatically email them two weeks ahead of time, saving on labor. Our automatic email message features "click here to confirm" box. That way we only need to follow up with those who don't respond online.

Be sure to ask for your clients' email addresses along with their permission to send them coupons or other special offers.

Asking for permission is vital. Your message is much more likely to be read by a customer who gave her email address voluntarily than by someone whose name you acquired by purchasing an email address list, in which case a spam filter likely will discard the message before the recipient ever sees it.

Appointment Confirmation

Be careful not to email too frequently. If you send too many messages, your customers may unsubscribe and you'll lose the advantage of a very low-cost mode of communication. Remember: moderation is key.

Texting is among the latest, most rapid forms of communication. Texting is now first in customer communication—ahead of email, websites, and social media. Over 90 percent of texts are read within ninety minutes. If I want my kids to come downstairs for dinner, I don't yell for them; they won't answer! But if I send them a text message, they're downstairs in seconds. Texting has become one of the best and most direct ways to contact your customers, and it gets the best response.

Apps on an iPhone are like magnets on a refrigerator.

Another perfect way to stay connected with your customers is to develop an app (short for "application"). When I was little, when my mom needed to call the physician, dentist, or pharmacist, she found the phone number on one of the many magnets posted on our refrigerator. The apps on today's smart phones are just like the magnets on my mother's refrigerator.

When we send our patients a message, a little red indicator pops up on their app button to alert them that they have a message from their dental office. Imagine if your dry cleaner offered you an app that let you know when your clothes were ready to pick up.

Again, take advantage of the latest technology in staying connected to your clients. Don't allow yourself to get comfortable with the same old ways of doing things. In the words of Charles Darwin: "It isn't the strongest of the species that survives, nor the most intelligent that survives. It is the one that is the most adaptable to change."

I am fifty years old. Over the past two decades, I have witnessed firsthand dental practices that achieved enormous success and others that slowly faded away. The difference was in whether or not they were willing to adapt to new technology.

The successful dentists "tweet" a holiday greeting to a thousand customers, followed by another tweet alerting them of the special promotion their practice is offering in the New Year.

Social media makes personal connections with your customers easy and effective. Learn to master social media! It is vital to stay connected with your customers and your colleagues, so put the time into Facebook, Twitter, Google+, LinkedIn, and Pinterest.

During World War II, four-star General George S. Patton told his men they weren't going to dig in like their opponents. He said if the American troops kept moving and taking risks, we would win the war. Patton and his troops made record time moving across Europe. When the enemy thought Patton and his men would arrive at a location in three days, Patton would get there in one and catch them with their pants down. He once moved his men one hundred miles through a snowstorm in a single day.

You need to lead like General Patton and keep advancing. You can't dig in and let someone overtake you. Spend more time engaging your customers in new ways to keep them coming back to you.

I'll give you an example. In my dental office we did a little experiment with sleep apnea and snore guards. We got into this area of dentistry after the mother of one of my staff members inquired about it. My associate Dr. Michael Glass and I attended a two-day sleep apnea course in Scottsdale, Arizona, where we learned how miserable it is for people who have to lie in bed next to a partner who snores all night. We became the dentists who got their partners to quit snoring, and our clients started telling the whole world about us. The number of word-of-mouth referrals we received was stunning, and all because we were doing something that touched and changed lives.

In your business, think about ways you can meet and exceed the expectations of your customers so they, too, become raving fans of who you are and what you do.

VALUE YOUR CLIENTS' FEEDBACK

Tell your clients, "We always love to hear comments and suggestions from our loyal customers."

Getting to Yes

Time	Day	Date

1. Hygiene appointment time available per request?   yes / no
2. Doctor appointment time available per request?   yes / no
3. Appointment time after 5 p.m. available?   yes / no
4. Appointment time after 9 a.m. available?   yes / no
5. Patient has HMO insurance?   yes / no
6. Patient has no insurance or money?   yes / no

Keep one eye on customer so you can create a supply of what your patients want, need and desire

Time to reorder? Call Farran Media 480-598-0001

I have a notepad that looks like an old prescription pad next to every telephone in my office. The title reads, "Getting to Yes." Not only do I want to hear feedback from my loyal customers, I want to track the demand for everything to which we say "No."

If customers call asking about our office hours and we aren't open during the hours they're requesting, I have to track that information. Business, in three words, is "Supply and Demand." I have to create a supply of what the people in my village are demanding and that has to be methodically tracked. I can't go by a gut feeling of what customers want; I need data, I need numbers. When we're considering joining a specific insurance plan, I need to know how often people are asking about it: once a year, once a month, once a week or once a day. I need all the data I can get to make a proper decision. I want to methodically track everything my customers demand. Ideally I want to figure out a way where I can profitably get to *yes*. If I can take a *no* and figure out how to make money turning it into a *yes*, that's free enterprise!

RESPECT YOUR CLIENTS' TIME

No matter what your business, your clients'—your customers'—time is valuable. If they feel you are wasting their time, they will go elsewhere. Respect your customers' time as much as your own. How do you do that? You work on making sure your processes are in order, your service is consistent, and you deal with problems correctly.

One of Ray Kroc's first innovations at McDonald's was replacing a single malt mixer with one that made five malts at once. Instead of waiting for their malts to be made one at a time, a family of five could be served in a matter of minutes, cutting the wait time for the next customer in line.

I borrowed this idea for my dental office twenty-five years ago. Nearly every mom who came in complained about the amount of time it took to bring her family in for a cleaning. First it's little Billy, then little Amy, then Mom, then Dad. The family would spend nearly half the day in the dental office. So when I started my practice, I employed three hygienists. While the first two hygienists spent an hour each cleaning Mom's and Dad's teeth, the third spent thirty minutes each on Billy and Amy. The family would come in at eight in the morning and leave together at nine.

While other dentists waited to hire additional hygienists until they thought they could afford to, I did so from day one. And word spread quickly that, at my practice, an entire family could get their teeth cleaned in one hour.

I know dentists who believe that the best way to cut overhead is to cut back on supplies. They believe they are saving money by only buying one of everything. They might be in the middle of a procedure and discover that one of the tools they need is still in the operatory down the hall, so the assistant has to stop and go get it.

The doctor who actually has low overhead knows her true cost is time and will invest in everything she needs for every operatory so that when she says "go," the assistant never needs to leave the room.

Occasionally, no matter how streamlined your process, you're going to run late. It happens and your customers will have to wait.

When you have to make your customers wait, make sure your staff follows the eight principles of waiting as developed by Harvard Business School professor David Maister:

1. *Unoccupied time feels longer than occupied time.* This is why you'll often find a window or a mirror beside a hotel elevator. Having something to look at makes the wait for the elevator to make its way down from the thirty-seventh floor seem less tedious.

2. *Pre-process waits feel longer than in-process waits.* I would rather sit at the table with my drink to wait for the server to come take my order, than stand out in front of the restaurant waiting to be seated. I would rather be waiting in the operatory in the dentist chair, waiting five times longer than necessary for my anesthetic to work, than twiddle my thumbs in the waiting room. I don't know it was ready a

full fifteen minutes ago; I actually think I'm doing something productive.

3. *Anxiety makes waits seem longer.* Depending on the nature of your profession or business, the issue of anxiety may or may not apply. In mine, I refer to this as, "putting on my mom hat." When they were little, my four boys could play with me for hours, but whenever they fell down and got hurt, they always ran to mom. Sometimes they'd run around me to get to mom to show her their booboo. When my patients are frustrated or scared, I always put on my mom hat. Like mom, I try to calm them down. Sometimes I'll put my hand on their shoulder or pat their hand and assure them: "It's going to be fine. I do this all day every day, and you're going to be just fine."

4. *Uncertain waits are longer than known, finite waits.* By telling a person exactly how long the wait is going to be, the wait doesn't seem as long; they can plan what they're going to do while they wait. Just let them know.

5. *Unexplained waits are longer than explained waits.* Your customers shouldn't have to stand there fuming and thinking you're incompetent. Just tell them what is going on. In most cases, they will understand.

6. *Unfair waits are longer than equitable waits.* There's nothing more annoying than when after you've been waiting to be seated for thirty minutes, someone else walks in the front door and gets seated right away. Don't ever let that happen.

7. *The more valuable the service, the longer I will wait.* Obviously people will wait longer for life-saving bypass surgery than they will for a taco at Taco Bell.

8. *Solo waiting feels longer than group waiting.* Make your waiting area fun and festive!

Source: The Psychology of Waiting Lines by David Maister (http://davidmaister.com/articles/the-psychology-of-waiting-lines/)

It's up to you to keep your customers from waiting. After all, their time is as valuable to them as your time is to you.

When a client does have to wait, your acknowledgement and apology are critical. You're human and so are they. So apologize and if it's appropriate, explain why you're late. Remember: Satisfaction = Perception – Expectations.

Make it a goal to spend quality time with all of your customers. Find a common bond. In his classic business book, *How to Win Friends and Influence People*, Dale Carnegie wrote that the way to bond with people is to talk only about them. Keep the focus and the conversation centered on them, not on you.

About a year ago my garage door broke. The repair company I called sent over a young man who appeared eager to get to know me, and we soon discovered we both grew up in the same Kansas area.

Should a problem come up with my garage door in the future, I'm going to call the same company and ask for the same serviceman, because I know he's going to do a good job and I feel like I know him.

Above all else, your clients want to feel valued. When you are communicating with them, they want to feel as though they are the most important people on earth, and it's your job to make them feel that way.

ACTION POINTS

- Take the time to get to know your customers.

- Ask your customers how you can improve your business for them.

- Reward every customer who refers you another customer, even if it's just with a phone call thanking them for the referral.

- Invest in whatever you need—whether it be supplies, equipment, or additional employees—to maximize your time efficiency for your customers.

- Develop strong digital connections with your customers via text messaging, email, your website, and social media such as Facebook, Twitter, LinkedIn, Pinterest, and Google+.
- Create a culture of methodically tracking customer feedback, both positive and in areas where you failed to meet or exceed your customers' expectations.
- Make sure everyone in your business understands the eight principles of waiting.

When you really matter to someone,
that person will always make time for you.
No excuses, no lies, and no broken promises.

—Anonymous

13

Technology

One day when economist and Nobel Prize winner Milton Friedman was visiting an Asian country, he accompanied a government official to a construction site where workers were building a canal with nothing more sophisticated than shovels. No tractors or machinery of any kind. When Friedman asked why they weren't using modern equipment, the official explained it allowed them to employ more workers. Friedman said, "Oh, I thought you were trying to build a canal. If it's jobs you want, then you should give these workers spoons, not shovels."

Although there are several versions of that story, the point is always the same; the belief that technology is fatal to employment is a fallacy.

Karl Marx, the father of communism, believed it. He said, "The production of too many useful things results in too many useless people." He believed automation would leave only useless, unemployed people in its wake.

However, the value of technology is the ability to make your workforce—always your largest expense category—more efficient and productive. Even when some form of technology replaces a worker, that only frees the worker to pursue bigger and better things.

For example in 1900, two-thirds of all the workers in America were in the agriculture business; today less than 2 percent of Americans are farmers. What happened to all those unemployed people? They became physicians, dentists, musicians, computer programmers, and pioneers of countless other professions that didn't even exist a hundred years ago. I tell my four boys that when they're my age, half the jobs in America will be in industries that have not yet been invented.

I love my iPhone—not because I'm a Steve Jobs devotee or an Apple nut, although I am, but because this technology made things so much easier for me. Just two simple applications—the calendar and the notepad—are the two most used buttons on my phone. Every night before I go to bed, I look at my calendar to see what I have scheduled for the next day. I also glance at my notepad that has just one heading: "To Do."

I don't love technology for its own sake. I love it for what it can do to help my business become more efficient and productive. In the words of Steve Jobs, "Innovation distinguishes between a leader and a follower."

EMBRACE TECHNOLOGY FOR PRODUCTIVITY

Technology is fundamental when looking at managing time, people, and money. What we desperately need is for employees and business owners to be able to get more done in the same unit of time. When it comes to managing time, 80 percent is technology and 20 percent is personal discipline.

If you want to be more productive, you need to be faster at what you do. There are so many different products, equipment, and technologies available to help a person work faster and be more productive.

Again, if your total overhead—your cost—is $1 a day and you do $1 in sales, your overhead is 100 percent and you're not making any profit. If you invest capital—money—in technology to make your $1 of cost and overhead now produce $2 a day, now your overhead just fell to 50 percent and you're as profitable as Microsoft, Intel, and Apple. The key to lowering your overhead is doing whatever you do faster, easier, and more efficiently, which will also make your product or service higher in quality and lower in cost. And you'll be on your way to getting rich.

Products, equipment, and technology are constantly improving through innovation. Innovation is the creation of a better or more effective idea, method, product, service, or technology. Necessity is the mother of all invention. It is necessary to lower your overhead.

How many times have you bought a new item or piece of equipment and within months, something new comes along that is significantly better, faster, easier, and lower in price? Look at the innovation in Apple products over the years. A company that started with a single personal computer now has a multitude of innovations. I wonder if the people who purchased the original Apple computer ever thought they would be able to carry that technology and then some in their pocket or briefcase.

The world of entertainment and music has forever changed through the innovations that Apple introduced with iPods and iTunes. Many of your grandkids and possibly some of your kids will never grasp the concept of having to physically drive down to the record store to buy that new record album. Instead they will just log onto iTunes, purchase, and download any song or album they want to their device within seconds. They will laugh at the fact that you actually had to flip over the record to hear the rest of the songs or the fact that you couldn't even listen to your favorite album in the car. The constant innovation of music technology has come a long way and will continue to change and innovate like all businesses should.

When Steve Jobs and Apple first introduced the iPod, Wall Street said, "Who cares? You're in the PC business." Yet Jobs was convinced his little iPod would sell more Apple computers than anything else to date. It was genius. That tiny Apple product turned consumers onto the Apple computer brand until eventually the consumer market shifted from Microsoft to Apple. Talk about building a billion-dollar brand!

Another company that continues to change, improve, and innovate is Intel. Intel introduced the world's first microprocessor in 1971. You won't see a single human being on the Intel processor chip assembly line; the chips are made entirely by machines. People are employed solely to maintain and calibrate the machinery. That's why Intel can make so many high quality chips. If humans were making chips by hand, the process would take much more time with a much greater margin of error. Robots rarely make errors. They are more efficient, faster, and more productive than humans doing the same job.

Early on, the people at Intel determined that robotic technology was what the company needed to grow and excel.

When I graduated from dental school in 1987, the method for doing a root canal was much different than it is today. (A root canal is necessary when the tiny canal in the middle of each tooth that houses the nerve, as well as carries blood and nutrients to the tooth, becomes infected.) The old method was to use a tiny, needle-thin, stainless steel hand file to clean out and sterilize the inside of the canal—a process that took up to three hours and often over the course of three one-hour appointments. For the first five years of my practice, I had permanent blisters on my thumb and index finger from those darn little files.

With technology came automatic files that either ultrasonically vibrated or automatically spun around at about 300 RPMs. The technology grew out of a metal developed by NASA. NASA discovered mixing titanium with metal resulted in a metal that would bend, but then spring back to its original shape. It was the first metal with memory. Once the dental industry started using this nickel titanium metal to make these automated files, a root canal that required three one-hour appointments took less than an hour. Not only did technology make me faster, it made the job easier at a lower cost, with higher quality and a better outcome for the patient. There was no way I could clean out that root canal by hand in three hours as well as I could do it with these new files.

This technology not only improved the way I performed that one procedure, it enabled me to overhaul my entire practice. With the additional time, I could see more patients, do more dentistry, and earn more income with the existing overhead, staff, and equipment. It also greatly increased patient satisfaction.

Be customer focused, not owner focused. For example, back when dentists used Kodak film for taking X-rays, I owned the X-ray and kept it for my records. I needed that X-ray to compare it to later X-rays to determine if there had been any changes. The patient depended solely on me to understand and explain what was going on inside her mouth.

With the development of digital X-rays, I can print an 8 × 10 inch copy of the patient's X-ray, circle the cavity with my red pen, and make any other pertinent notes, and the patient comes away with the same information and understanding as I have. The technology has made my business much more customer focused.

GO PAPERLESS

Going digital in our office also included transitioning to a paperless office. I was among the first practices to go paperless in 1999. I can hardly believe that, twelve years later, so many of the dental practices in America still haven't done it!

We used to have eight thousand patient charts filled with X-rays, legal consent forms, insurance forms, and letters from other physicians. After ten years, a patient of ours had a chart a half-inch thick. As the dentist, I would have to leaf through all the papers and look at dozens of old X-rays, just to find what I was looking for. To make matters worse, not a day went by without a chart getting lost. Every single day someone spent thirty minutes looking for a chart that was either mis-placed or misfiled.

Today my office stores everything digitally. So instead of taking up an entire room, all of our information is stored on one server. Every computer in the office has access to all the files, patient charts, and X-rays through our practice management software. We no longer need to worry about misfiling or misplacing a patient's chart. Because all the notes and patient information are typed directly into the program software, the information is always clean, legible, and can all be found in one location. By going paperless, you will never need to bear the consequences of lost or inaccurate paperwork.

Office manager at Today's Dental

One of the measures you can take to go paperless is direct deposit. Do you still print or write out payroll checks to your employees? Many banking institutions offer direct deposit and payroll services for small businesses. Direct deposit is not only beneficial for you, the business owner, but your employees also will appreciate the convenience. With direct deposit there are no physical checks to be lost or stolen, thus you never have to take time reissuing a check. It saves your employees a trip to the bank and gives them the assurance that, even if they are out of town or sick, their check will still reach their account on payday.

Direct deposit also reduces the risk of fraud by ensuring the check is deposited directly into the employee's account. With direct deposit you control the date of withdrawal from your account. By having your banking numbers all digital, all online, and perhaps even on an app on your smartphone, you will find yourself reviewing them more often, allowing you to catch any problems immediately.

Transitioning to a paperless office has a number of benefits:

- It makes communication more efficient. Putting everything on the computer streamlines the communication process. Everything is easy to look for and easy to find.

- It lowers your overhead by allowing each employee to get more done.

- It reduces errors. When my office filled out insurance forms by hand, and the insurance companies then manually input the data, nearly every insurance claim contained some error. Now that we're paperless, the form is filled out online and sent directly to the insurance company where is goes directly into their system.

Sam Walton, founder of Wal-Mart, revolutionized retail when he rented space on a government satellite to connect his cash registers in Bentonville, Arkansas, to his suppliers. If you walked into Sam Walton's store in 1962 and bought a Barbie doll, Mattel© knew immediately and began shipment of a new Barbie to replace the one you just bought. No errors. No humans involved. No high costs. Just fast, easy, and efficient. Sam Walton did this with such a cost advantage in 1962 that he drove his top competitors out of business.

PREPARE FOR THE CLOUD

And by this, I don't mean save for a rainy day. We've already established the importance of investing in your business.

I'm talking about "cloud computing." Cloud computing is the latest stage in the Internet's evolution, combining all the hardware, networks, storage, services, and interfaces to give you access to all of your information wherever and whenever you need it.

The concept is similar to the evolution of electricity. In the early days, if you wanted electricity, you had to make your own. You built a fire using wood or coal to burn the water to create the stream to turn the turbine to generate enough electricity to fuel your light bulb. Thanks to Nicola Tesla and his contributions to the design of the alternating current (AC) electricity supply system, electricity was generated in a single power plant where it was then sold and delivered to the consumer.

That is the same concept behind the cloud. All you want is your data; you don't need to know or care about all that goes into storing and delivering it. You don't need to learn how to link to a network, backup data, install a firewall—or even hire an Information Technology (IT) expert who does. With cloud computing, Google and Amazon will do all that for you. As long as you have an Internet connection, you can put all of your software on the cloud and gain access to it no matter where you are on the planet.

As a business owner, you don't want to be the 21st century equivalent of the guy shoveling coal into a burner in the middle of the night just so he can turn on his lights. It is estimated that cloud computing will save the world $1 trillion a year. When the stakes are that high, trust me, we're all going to the cloud. In fact, if you use Gmail, your email is already stored on the cloud. Every video on YouTube is already stored on the cloud. Your business potentially could save a fortune in IT costs by moving all your software to the cloud where it will be stored, backed up, protected, and instantly accessible. Software engineers with PhDs manage everything behind the scenes, around the clock.

Currently more than 2,000 companies exist solely on the cloud. Right now, you can run almost every business entirely on the cloud.

ANALYZE YOUR USE OF TECHNOLOGY

Take a walk around your business and look for the ways you can increase your efficiency and productivity with technology. What new digital technology can you utilize? What type of upgrades can you make? What can you buy to help your staff's work become faster, easier, and higher in quality?

Spending the money now will save you money later, especially with labor. Think of it this way: between what you take home and what all your employees take home from your business, an average of 50 percent of your money is going to you and your people. Instead of spending a little—1 or 2 percent of sales—on technology, invest in the technology that will make your expensive staff as efficient and productive as possible. The more efficient your employees, the lower your labor costs, and the higher your net income. As a business owner you need to stay up to date technologically to continue to be successful.

Don't be afraid of technology; embrace it!

ACTION POINTS

- Analyze your current use of technology and determine what you can add or upgrade to increase your employees' productivity and the quality of your product or service. Ask your employees for their ideas on any technology or equipment that would make their jobs faster, easier, and higher in quality.
- Go paperless wherever possible.

It's not a faith in technology.
It's faith in people.

—Steve Jobs

Hire a Consultant

Consultants exist because they work. Modern day economies are so efficient that people who don't provide value for the price usually don't stay in business very long. Many entrepreneurs are arrogant because they know what they know and they know they're "successful."

Yet as I like to say, *you know what you know, but you don't know what you don't know.* You live inside your business. You know everything about your business. What consultants bring to the table is the knowledge they have gained from observing scores of businesses within your vertical. What works and what doesn't work tend to trend across a sector.

After twenty-five years as a dentist, I can easily identify a list of key differences between the behavior of a dentist making $300,000 and that of a dentist making $100,000.

For example, the dentist doing $300,000 a year designates a specific employee to present the treatment plan to each patient, while the dentist making $100,000 does it herself. The dentist doing $300,000 has two or three hygienists doing all the cleanings, while the $100,000 dentist does the cleanings herself. The $300,000 dentist usually has office hours that start before eight in the morning, extend beyond five in the afternoon and include time on Saturdays. The $100,000 dentist is only open Monday through Thursday from eight to five.

Another critical difference between these two dentists is the willingness to pay for a consultant.

Recently I sat with a couple of dentists during lunch break at a dental meeting. They were commiserating, sharing war stories from "the front." I figured the two were good friends, because they were talking about some major problems they were having in their offices. One dentist asked the other how her office scheduled patients, admitting that his days contained a host of frustrations. There was no rhyme or reason to how his scheduling coordinator organized his day. His practice's production was nowhere near where he thought it should be.

The other dentist listened and then recommended he hire a consultant.

It took me the first two years of running my practice to realize I didn't know it all. Although my team and I had already doubled our annual income, I brought in Sally McKenzie, a consultant specific to dentistry to help me streamline my management systems. I knew it was the only way to bring my business to the point where I could reach my goals and thoroughly enjoy going to work everyday.

Her experience proved invaluable. I lived all day long in my dental practice, while Sally lived in up to a hundred dental offices day in and day out, year after year. She enabled me to look at my practice more objectively by telling me what worked and did not work for all those other offices.

Years later I brought in top consultant Sandy Pardue who took my already successful business to even higher levels.

I cannot stress this enough; the service of a consultant is time wise and cost efficient.

Every Fortune 500 company employs lots of MBAs. These same companies also routinely have a convoy of outside consultants tweaking every little aspect of their businesses. The inside MBAs know that the return on investment from the outside MBAs is usually positive. If it wasn't, the outside MBAs couldn't stay in business. Every business can benefit from a third-party onlooker—from an unbiased, uninvolved, but educated perspective. Often consultants are able to see the discrepancies between being busy and being productive.

Consider your own business. Aside from simply feeling things should be better, there are a number of tangible indicators that could benefit your business were you to bring in a consultant: increasing sales and customer retention, as well as reducing your overhead and employee turnover.

Perhaps you are missing specific measurements to evaluate your employees' performance, or your bonus and reward systems are not targeting the specific actions and behaviors you're looking for. Perhaps your current job descriptions need clarification.

A consultant can help you with all this and much more. Consultants can save you time and money.

ACTION POINTS

- Identify the top three consultants in your vertical.
- Meet with the top three consultants in your vertical for a no-obligation interview.
- Invest in a consultant for a one-year trial.
- Listen closely to what the consultant says, but recognize the final decision on what is best for your business belongs to you. Always stay true to yourself.

When you change the way you look at things,
the things you look at change.

—*Wayne Dyer*

Summary

A s the song by the Rolling Stones goes, *time is on my side.* Time can be on your side, too. Remember, the more systems you have in place and the more technology you can utilize, the quicker and more seamlessly your business will operate, and the more time you will have to spend on the factors that make your business profitable.

I am easily satisfied by the very best.

—*Winston Churchill*

SECTION III

MONEY

Introduction

As we've discussed, running a business doesn't have to be complicated if you focus on three things: people, time, and money. Here's an example of a business that missed the mark on the third item.

A new restaurant opened up near my home in Phoenix, Arizona. They had been marketing in my area pretty strongly—billboards, advertisements in the local shopper, and direct mail cards with "free dessert" coupons. Almost everywhere you turned, something displayed this restaurant's name. I'm a creature of habit, so despite all the advertising, I hadn't really considered going until a close friend of mine recommended it.

I took my family on a Thursday night. It was a pretty place, with a pleasant atmosphere, and the food was pretty decent. And the place was bustling. The friendly and helpful staff hurried from table to table, waiting on diners as fast as possible so they could seat the people who had been waiting up front for an hour. It really seemed as though this place would take off.

The manager came around to my table and asked me how I liked my meal and if I was enjoying myself. I told her everything was great, but that I was curious to know how many new customers her restaurant was getting each month.

She appeared dumbfounded at first, but then she finally said: "I don't know. Probably around fifty?" The woman had no idea.

I just let it go and decided I'd wait and see how things were going with this restaurant in a few months.

My favorite restaurant happens to be located across the street from this place. It is one of four restaurants in my zip code that has stayed in business for all twenty-five years I have lived there. I know the managers of all four, and they know me.

So one night when I was dining at my favorite restaurant, I asked the manager how many new customers he attracts in a month. He said, "On average, about forty, but last month we had forty-two."

When I asked where his new customers came from, he said, "Well, five came from our website, ten came from a Google ad, twenty were word of mouth referrals" . . . He went on down the list.

This guy didn't even have to check his data. He knew it cold. He even knew how many dollars per head his new customers cost him in advertising on his website, direct mail, Facebook, and in the newspaper. Why? Because he wanted to invest his money where he was getting the most bang for his buck. He was measuring his return on investment. A classic entrepreneur.

Eventually that other restaurant went out of business. When once no one could get in, now no one wanted to go. It was a shame, really, but I saw it coming from a mile away. Management cared more about how its "product" was made than about watching the numbers. If you're not passionate about running your business *and* watching your numbers, it won't matter whether you're making crowns, pizzas, or depositions, because you won't have a business at which to make it!

This section is about watching the numbers. Since, as a business owner, you only manage people, time, and money, you need to learn to love to watch the numbers. That is why I went back to school to get my MBA. I realized that if I'm going to succeed and run a $10 million company some day—and eventually a $100 million company—then I needed training. Getting my MBA was the single best business decision I ever made, but you don't need an MBA to know you need to watch your numbers.

Money not only fuels your business, it also allows you to measure your success. Attaching numbers to the goals you've set for your business enables you to progress towards your goals in a specific way.

It is important to remember, however, that while money is a tool for measuring your goals, you should never make money a goal in itself. Keep that in mind and you'll run a successful business.

So let's talk numbers.

If winning isn't everything,
why do they keep score?

—*Vince Lombardi*

Watch the Numbers at Home

Millionaires become millionaires not because of what they make, but because of what they save. You don't need to be a genius to understand that if you spend more than you make, you'll end up broke. The world has plenty of broke geniuses. Yet too many of us live on credit, paying high interest rates to Visa and MasterCard for stuff we "have to have now" but soon lose interest in. It's a sickness. Chances are if you run your personal finances that way, you'll do the same with your business. Knock it off. If you spend more money than you make, you'll never build your savings account, never have any real access to investment capital and never have enough money to retire.

A healthy financial life begins at home. The most stressful marriages I've ever seen are those in which both partners are spenders. They pull money out of an ATM machine like it's a winning slot machine in Vegas and rack up major credit card debt, only to end up fighting over where all the money is going.

Learning to save leads to a low-stress life.

MAKE TOUGH DECISIONS ABOUT YOUR PERSONAL SPENDING

To fully understand the importance of numbers, you need to take a step back. Reexamine your personal life and your personal financial goals. I tire of listening to fellow dentists complain that their practices are failing, that they can't afford to undertake a marketing campaign to attract new patients, while they live in mansions and are willing to lease a Mercedes-Benz at a thousand dollars a month.

If this is you, take a good look at yourself in the mirror. Why aren't you making the tough decisions? Are you concerned about how your stay-at-home spouse will react if you say it's time to rein in your household spending and to get a job? Are you afraid that downsizing your house and trading in your BMW for a practical car will cost you your high-class image?

Put your Rolex up for auction on eBay, and you might pick up a couple thousand dollars along with the revelation that you've invested too much money in needless *stuff*. To borrow a line from the movie, *Fight Club*: "The things you own end up owning *you*." You don't need the boat. You don't need the vacation condo, the fancy cars, or the membership to the country club. You can't afford to go out to eat four nights a week. You need to sit down and figure out how to cut your personal expenses, because they're also eating into your business's bottom line. Seriously, how good does it feel that you bought your wife that Gucci purse or your husband a new Rolex watch? That's $5,000 that you could have reinvested in your business. You could have built a new website for your business for what you dropped on a fancy handbag or watch.

MAKE TOUGH DECISIONS ABOUT SPENDING ON YOUR FAMILY

I've heard other professionals say they are about to literally go broke from the cost of putting their kids through college.

Here's what I say: "Why?" You aren't doing yourself, your business and, especially, your children any favors. What is the downside to allowing your children to learn the value of achieving goals on their own? I was on my own in college; I made it, and I was a better person for it. I would put all of my eggs into the basket of a self-made man over one who was born with a silver spoon in his mouth. Be honest; wouldn't you?

Your first measurement, your first consideration, in gauging your success is straightforward: Do you spend more than you save? If so, stop it. Get out of debt immediately. Until your personal numbers are in order, you will not be able to get your business numbers in order.

Money is nothing more than a yardstick, a way to measure your progress. However, measuring is useless unless you have something to measure against. When setting your financial goals, all you need to remember is that whatever gets measured gets managed.

The best way to ensure you're heading in the right direction is through measurement. Consider weight loss, for instance. I read an interesting study in which the researcher compared two groups of people on the same weight loss program. The members of one group weighed in every day, wrote down the result and posted it where they could see it; the members of the other group had no specific requirement for tracking their weight. That was the only variable in the study.

After one hundred days, the group who weighed in daily lost a higher percentage of weight than the group that did not.

Makes sense, right? If you stepped on the scale in the morning and your first reaction was, "Dude, I need to lose some weight," don't you think you'd be more likely to make higher quality decisions about your nutrition and fitness? When you sit down at the restaurant for lunch, you might think, "Okay, this morning I was up to 220 pounds, so I had better not get the bacon cheeseburger."

Watching your numbers begins at home. Then you are ready to carry the process into your business.

- Don't spend more money than you earn. Save.
- Understand that managing your personal finances is the first step in managing your business finances.
- Avoid spending for personal consumption.
- Review the financial goals you established in the first section of this book.
- See whether or not you are in line with your established goals.
- Adjust your spending budget.

Economy does not lie in sparing money,
but in spending it wisely

—Thomas Huxley

Watch Your Business Numbers

Once you have your personal numbers in order, it's time to focus on your business numbers. Rule Number 1 is the same for both: *Don't overspend.*

Do you have the money in your budget to buy that new piece of equipment? Do you know your average monthly production for this year as compared to last year? What is your accounts receivable? Do you know your collection percentage? Do you know how many new customers you are seeing on a monthly basis? Do you know what percentage of your income you are spending on supplies, labor, rent, advertising, equipment, and utilities each month? Do you know your daily, weekly, and monthly break-even point (BEP)? Do you know how much money you need to make just to break even? Do you know what time of day you reach your BEP and enter the profit zone?

The answer to all of these questions should be, "Yes!" If not, then get with the program and figure it out. The future of your business depends on it. Otherwise you might find yourself filing for bankruptcy.

Think of how many well-known actors, musicians, and artists go bankrupt. Francis Ford Coppola, producer of the *Godfather* movies, nearly always came in over budget and ended up filing for Chapter 11. Sarah "Fergie" Ferguson, the Duchess of York, went into debt for more than $7 million. MC Hammer filed for bankruptcy and then put his multi-million-dollar, twenty-room mansion up for sale. Kim Basinger bought a town in Georgia and then was sued for breach of contract. Toni Braxton, a six-time Grammy winner who has sold millions of albums, has gone bankrupt—twice—after entering into raw deals with recording companies and tying up her own capital in unproven entertainment ventures.

Even Ulysses S. Grant, the highest ranking general in the Civil War and our country's eighteenth president, went broke for living way above his means and entering into a mismanaged investment venture that sent his partner to prison and left Grant hundreds of thousands of dollars in debt. The only thing that saved his family from even more hardship was selling his memoirs for about $500,000.

Either these talented, accomplished individuals went broke because they were not watching the numbers, or the person they paid to watch the numbers looked away.

I see this in dentistry all the time. Walk into almost any dental practice and ask, "How many new patients did you get last month?" and chances are, they won't know. Ask for more complex information such as, "How much did it cost you to get a new patient?" and all you're likely to get back are blank stares.

I know that every one of my new patients costs about $100 if I get them from a Google ad, $100 if they come from 1-800-DENTIST, $250 if they come from direct mail and $400 back when we advertised in the Yellow Pages. In my office, we've always measured *everything*.

Can you imagine driving your car without your dashboard measurements? You're driving down the highway, thinking you've got enough gas to get from point A to point B, but the car sputters and dies because there was no gauge to let you know you had run out. Or maybe your radiator overheats because you had no temperature gauge. Without the car dashboard, we'd probably all be using public transportation a whole lot more.

If a business owner knows all of her numbers, she will have the information she needs to know when to speed up or slow down. Businesses get into trouble when they spend all of their time working on the product and not on the business.

Even those business owners who realize they need to do a better job of watching their numbers may turn their attention to them again for a week or so, but then go right back to doing whatever they were doing.

Make watching your numbers a personal, life-long habit.

There is really one very simple trick to watching your numbers and that is simply:

WATCH YOUR NUMBERS!

Most entrepreneurs and business owners are excited about their newest service or the next transaction they're going to make, but if I asked you what your revenues were last quarter, you'd probably shrug and say, "Let me get back to you." I can't stress this enough: *You need to learn to love this part of your business as much as you love making your product or providing your service.* Unless you do, it almost doesn't matter what you're making—especially if you don't have the revenue to do it.

Require your staff to give you reports on a daily, weekly, and monthly basis and *really look at them*! Keeping your reports in a stack on your desk without looking at them is like holding a gym membership to your forehead and expecting to lose weight! It's just not going to happen. Eighty percent of working out is simply showing up. The only bad workout is the one you *didn't* do. It's the same with business; you have to put the time and effort into reviewing your numbers.

At my dental practice, we *review* and *balance* production and collections on a daily basis. We also set weekly and monthly production goals that we review to gauge how we are doing. On a monthly basis we also review our financial statements.

We'll go into all of this in more detail, but in brief, your financial statements will provide a snapshot of how your business is doing and should be looked at regularly.

I don't care if you're a Fortune 500 company or a small business on Main Street, fifty cents of every dollar you make goes toward paying people. After factoring in the rest of the overhead (supplies, rent, power, etc.), it's amazing how much of a dollar can get whittled away. Yet the great companies always take a small percentage of whatever is left from that dollar and reinvest it back into the company. You need to make it a goal to reinvest at least a nickel of every dollar you make back into your company.

Earn. Save. Reinvest. Watch the numbers. Those are the basics of sound money management.

Why You Need to Watch the Numbers
by Stacie Holub, Controller

I've been working with Dr. Farran for more than twelve years. I started in his accounting department as the bookkeeper handling payables and receivables for his three companies. His consistent passion and vision, along with an incredible staff, have allowed us to grow quite successfully even in some not-so-successful economic times.

Currently we have ten different entities and, as the controller, I'm the one closest to the financial pulse of our organization. Watching the cash flow each and every day comes as naturally to me as breathing. But given the amount of money flowing in and out daily, communication with my team and Dr. Farran, the owner, is critical.

Three key factors make for a healthy financial environment within a business. First, no person in a position working with incoming and outgoing money should ever be allowed to perform all the duties themselves, no matter how long they have been employed or what relationship they may have with you. Just knowing that checks and balances are in place assures the staff that the person in charge of the money (in this case, me) has no room to do anything unethical or improper.

Second, the entire staff should know "the Score": the business's financial picture. We keep these numbers in public files on the company server to encourage open communication among the staff, give them the peace of mind of knowing where the company stands, and keep motivation high. Transparency with the numbers encourages staff to monitor expenses and enables us to work together in planning for future needs.

Last, a solid collection policy is critical to a healthy cash flow, especially come payroll time.

As I said, I've been with Dr. Farran for many years. He should be able to trust me; he definitely can and does. Yet, should he trust me blindly? No!

As a business owner, you need to trust your staff. At the same time your staff needs to trust you to be the best owner you can be, and that means keeping your eye on the numbers and creating internal controls that protect both you and them.

ACTION POINTS

- WATCH YOUR NUMBERS! It's the most important function of business—more important than making and selling your product or service. Figure out your BEP on a daily, weekly, and monthly basis.

- Commit to reviewing numbers on a regular basis and make time in your schedule to do this—daily, weekly, monthly, quarterly, and yearly.
- Commit to reinvesting in your company on a regular basis.

The investor's chief problem—
and even his worst enemy—is likely to be himself.

—Benjamin Graham

Know the Important
Numbers to Watch

L et's get down to specifics. Exactly what numbers should you be watching?

Every business is different, even in the same market; even the spreadsheets for Nike and Reebok are going to look different from one another.

I use three basic business reports to track my numbers: statement of income, balance sheet, and statement of cash flow.

STATEMENT OF INCOME

Here is the formula that serves as the basis for your statement of income:

$$\text{Total Revenue} - \text{Total Expenses} = \text{Net Profit}$$

Statement of Income	Month Ending December 2012	%	Year to Date 2012	%
Income				
Patient Income	102,229	100.0%	1,030,867	100.0%
Patient Refunds	(1,974)	-1.9%	(6,591)	-0.6%
Other Income	0		0	
Total Income	100,255	98.1%	1,024,276	99.4%
Operating Expenses-Variable				
Dentists Wages	10,519	10.3%	69,826	6.8%
Hygienist Wages	11,537	11.3%	108,244	10.5%
Paradental Wages	8,234	8.1%	74,779	7.3%
Front Off Wages	6,413	6.3%	56,624	5.5%
Sub Total Hygiene/Paradental/Off	26,184	25.6%	239,647	23.2%
Sub Total All Wages	36,703	35.9%	309,473	30.0%
Lab Fees	8,209	8.0%	93,222	9.0%
Dental Supplies	6,601	6.5%	58,009	5.6%
Total Operating Expenses-Variable	51,513	50.4%	460,704	44.7%
Operating Expenses-Fixed				
Marketing Expenses	567	0.6%	6,583	0.6%
Other Operating Expenses	7,319	7.2%	75,002	7.3%
Facility Expenses	10,307	10.1%	71,712	7.0%
S G & A Expenses	1,697	1.7%	26,241	2.5%
Total Operating Expenses-Fixed	19,890	19.5%	179,538	17.4%
Total Operating Expenses	71,403	69.8%	640,242	62.1%
Owner Wages	22,313	21.8%	193,380	18.8%
Owner Payroll Taxes	3,070	3.0%	12,625	1.2%
Owner Professional Expenses	11,710	11.5%	65,757	6.4%
Retirement plan Contributions	2,500	2.4%	30,000	2.9%
Owner wages, Prof Exp. & Pension	39,593	38.7%	301,762	29.3%
Depreciation & Amort Expense	3,714	3.6%	31,577	3.1%
Interest Expense	806	0.8%	11,444	1.1%
Depreciation and Interest Expense	4,520	4.4%	43,021	4.2%
Net Income	(15,261)	-14.9%	39,251	3.8%

REVENUE

Revenue is often used interchangeably with *income*. It is the money received in your business from sales or service—from whatever your business provides.

EXPENSES

Expenses fall under two categories: *variable* and *fixed*.

Variable

Variable expenses, also referred to as *Cost of Goods Sold* (COGS), go up and down depending on your sales. They increase when you have more sales and decrease when you have fewer sales. For example, in a dental practice, variable expenses include labor, labs, and supplies; in a publishing company these costs would include labor, paper, printing, and postage.

Fixed

Fixed expenses do not go up or down based upon how busy you are. They are the expenses you pay each month whether you see one customer or a hundred. These include rent, mortgage, utilities (gas and electricity), insurance, computer software, professional dues, fees from lawyers and accountants, advertising, and marketing.

NET PROFIT

Net profit is your bottom line. Yes, you're in business because you have a passion, a purpose, and a goal, but to quote the Joker in the movie, *The Dark Knight*: "If you're good at something, never do it for free." You're in business to make money, and you aren't going to make any money if you find that you're spending more than you're bringing in.

Net profit is the amount of profit after *all* expenses have been deducted from the revenue. Here's a simple example:

Revenue	$1,000
Variable costs	$450, 45% (Labor, supplies, etc.)
Fixed costs	$150, 15% (Rent, equipment, insurance, etc.)
Net Profit	$400, 40% net profit margin

Another way to examine your profit is to look at your **net profit margin**, which is determined by $\frac{(Net)income}{revenue} \times 100$.

Your net profit margin is your percentage of profits. This is where benchmarking comes in handy. I'll explain benchmarking in more detail later on, but for now just know that it means to evaluate your business by comparing it to others within your industry. If the average net profit in your industry is 15 percent, but yours is only 5 percent, you are not managing your business as well as the competition in your vertical. If you want to be the frontrunner, you need to increase your profit margin.

As you review your statement of income, keep in mind that it does not paint the entire picture. You also have to look at your overall expenses—the money going out of your business. The statement of income—also referred to as the profit and loss statement or P&L—does not reflect some of the expenses that go toward any assets, liabilities, or taxes. These items are displayed on your balance sheet.

The statement also shows deferred taxes and depreciation because the statement of income is used primarily for the interests of a third party, such as the Internal Revenue Service when paying your taxes, or the Securities and Exchange Commission (SEC) if your business is publicly traded.

BALANCE SHEET

The balance sheet tells you the financial status of your business. It contains three categories:

- Assets: What your business <u>owns</u>
- Liabilities: What your business <u>owes</u>
- Equity: The <u>net value</u> of your business

Balance Sheet	As of November 30, 2012	As of December 31, 2012
ASSETS		
Current Assets		
Checking Account	13,843	1,102
Savings Acct	0	0
Total Current Assets	13,843	1,102
Property and Equipment		
Land	0	0
Today's Dental Building	0	0
Accumulated Depreciation	0	0
Dental Equipment	227,631	227,631
Accumulated Depreciation	(203,237)	(205,619)
Office Equipment(Furn & Fixt)	48,432	48,432
Accumulated Depreciation	(46,076)	(46,171)
Computer Equipment	9,650	9,650
Accumulated Depreciation	(9,650)	(9,650)
Computer Software	2,350	2,350
Accumulated Depreciation	(2,350)	(2,350)
Remodel-T&I Work	119,572	119,572
Accumulated Depreciation	(65,397)	(65,800)
Goodwill	105,000	105,000
Accumulated Amortization	(28,584)	(29,167)
Covenant n/t Compete	45,000	45,000
Accumulated Amortization	(12,250)	(12,500)
Total Property and Equipment	190,091	186,378
Other Assets		
Space Lease Deposit	1,884	1,884
Utility Deposit	0	0
	1,884	1,884
Total Assets	205,818	189,364
LIABILITIES AND CAPITAL		
Current Liabilities		
401k/PS plan payable	29,050	33,387
Due To Shareholder	0	1,120
Credit Card Payable	0	0
Total Current Liabilities	29,050	34,507
Long-Term Liabilities		
Bank Line of Credit - M&T	15,505	14,505
2010 Expansion Loan - M&T	152,373	149,223
Due TO Shareholder-LTD	0	0
Total Long-Term Liabilities	167,878	163,728
Total Liabilities	196,928	198,235
Capital		
Quarterly Profit Distribution	(27,690)	(30,190)
Capital Stock	1,000	1,000
Retained Earnings	(18,932)	(18,932)
Net Income	54,512	39,251
Total Capital	8,890	(8,871)
Total Liabilities & Capital	205,818	189,364
	205,818	189,364

The balance sheet follows the same formula you would use to calculate the equity in your home:

$$\text{Assets} - \text{Liabilities} = \text{Equity}$$

Example: If your home is worth \$100,000 and you owe \$80,000, your equity is \$20,000.

Similar to expenses, assets and liabilities each are separated into two categories.

ASSETS (CURRENT / FIXED)

Assets are either *current* or *fixed*. *Current assets* are your bank accounts, accounts receivable, and any notes owed to your business. *Fixed assets* include equipment, furniture, fixtures, and any land or building you own for your business.

LIABILITIES (CURRENT / LONG-TERM)

Liabilities are either *current* or *long term*. *Current liabilities* include payroll taxes, suppliers and credit card balances. *Long-term liabilities* include leases, mortgages, and loans.

EQUITY

Equity is the difference between assets that you own and liabilities that you owe.

The balance sheet provides a snapshot of your business's financial status at any given point in time.

A balance sheet lets you know exactly how much your business is worth and how much of that you own. A balance sheet is a report you run for the banker when you apply for a loan, or for your spouse when dividing assets in a divorce.

STATEMENT OF CASH FLOW

Cash flow is the movement of money in and out of your business. It is for managerial accounting and is the most important report to managing your business.

Statement of Cash Flow	Month Ending December 2012	Year To Date 2012
Beginning cash balance (from bank account)	13,843	7,396
Net Income \ (loss)	(15,261)	39,251
Adjustments to reconcile net income to net cash:		
Depreciation\Amortization	3,714	31,577
Net cash provided (used) from operations	2,296	78,224
Adjustments to reconcile net income to net cash:		
Changes in capital assets and liabilities\debts		
(Increase) decrease in Capital assets		
Employee Advances	0	0
Other Current Assets	0	0
Furniture and Equipment - Purchased	0	(1,181)
Increase (decrease) in liabilities\Debts		
401k/PS plan payable	4,336	(57)
Due To Shareholder	1,120	1,120
Credit Card Payable	(1,000)	(10,531)
2010 Expansion Loan	(3,150)	(36,283)
Quarterly Profit Distribution	(2,500)	(30,190)
Net Change in cash	1,102	1,102
Ending cash balance (from bank account) (should match Net Change in Cash above)	1,102	1,102

This is a very important number to watch. Running out of cash means it's curtains for your business. I advise tracking cash flow on a regular weekly basis to ensure you always have cash to work with. As shown in the example above, I run this report from my accounting software (I use Peachtree, although Quickbooks Pro by Intuit is excellent, as well). Once that number hits zero (or worse, in the red) you're in trouble.

If you can't pay your bills on time, you have cash flow issues and you immediately need to look at A) your prices and your collections policy, or B) what you are spending to produce what you make. In my MBA class at ASU, I learned 90 percent of the businesses that go bankrupt in the United States actually were *profitable*. Most companies don't go out of business because they were based on a bad idea or had a lazy management team. They failed simply because they ran out of cash. Here's an example:

Let's say I'm a farmer and I sell you $1,000 worth of tomatoes. My profit and loss statement reports that I made 10 percent profit on that sale. I'm scheduled to bill you in ninety days. However, within those ninety days I can't pay *my* bills, so I am forced to go bankrupt. On paper, my business was profitable, because when you paid me in ninety days, I would have made a $100 profit on selling you that $1,000 worth of tomatoes. But I am never going to see that $100 profit because I am not able to pay my labor, supplies, marketing, equipment, and utilities. My profitable business just went under because I didn't have ninety days worth of cash to carry me while I was waiting for you to pay. Again, the key is not only *how much* you charge, but *when* you collect.

The housecleaning business I use for my home once did not give me a bill for a full seven months, and then only because I specifically asked for one! I encountered a similar situation with my landscaping service that did not charge me for three full months of service. I can't imagine how either one will manage to stay in business.

Even in dentistry, practices go bankrupt all the time. Like so many other businesses, dental practices generally are very simple, small, and greatly needed in the marketplace. The only animals on earth that get cavities are humans and brown bears. Why? Because Winnie the Pooh eats honey and the average American eats 150 pounds of sugar a year. And, for the most part, neither animal brushes or flosses. So dentistry is needed around the world, yet dentists go bankrupt all the time and mainly for one reason: they simply run out of cash.

So what's the solution? Most bankruptcies could be avoided by doing two things: first, by maintaining a $10,000 floor—meaning keeping a minimum of $10,000 in the business checking account. *Always.* Any amount under that puts a small family business in the danger zone.

Second, to be and *stay* successful, every successful business needs a line of credit (LOC) with a bank. The time to establish a line of credit is *before* you start your business—not when you find yourself running out of cash. If you start your business on a Hail Mary because it was the only way you could do it, I can appreciate and understand your tenacity. But as soon as that business gets up and running, you have to work closely with your local banker.

I've had a twenty-five year relationship with one branch manager at Chase bank. I make certain to prioritize and continually monitor my line of credit and always seek to increase it. I'm always trying to maximize my line of credit. It's my insurance policy! What if something unforeseen happened? Look at 9/11! How many businesses in downtown Manhattan closed their doors? Floods, hurricanes, tornadoes, earthquakes, labor disputes . . . You never know what's going to happen.

You must keep a line of credit. When your bank account falls below the $10,000 floor, that's when you really need it. Most dentists I know don't even ask for help until they've overdrawn their account by $10,000, $20,000 or even $30,000! And when you go looking for a line of credit when you're already overdrawn $10,000 or more, that raises so many red flags for a bank, they'll never give it to you. Establishing a line of credit at the start of your business shows the bank you are preparing to manage any problems long before they occur.

Another reason you need that line of credit is for times when a major competitor goes bankrupt, opening an opportunity for a merger and acquisition.

Let's say something horrible happens at the dental practice across the street from me. Maybe the dentist lost his license due to alcohol or drugs, or had a heart attack and died. The next thing I know, that dental office across the street is for sale, *now,* and they're in no position to negotiate. I can go over there, make a cash offer and move all the customers from one of my major competitors over to my practice. Without a line of credit, however, I'd lose that opportunity.

Without any line of credit, you might not even know whether buying out a competitor is something you *could* do. And while you're at the bank trying to figure that out, another one of your competitors swoops in and buys the business out from under you.

A great reason just to seek a line of credit is to benefit from your banker's analysis of your business. If a banker turns down your request for a line of credit, listen to the reasons why. Maybe your debt is too high, your personal consumption is too high, and your profit margin is too small. Getting turned down for a line of credit can be a great exercise in learning where your business and personal management need to improve.

Success doesn't mean you never fall down; it means that you always get back up.

If you take nothing else away from this chapter, I hope it's this: by simply following the $10,000 floor rule and maintaining your line of credit, you drastically reduce your chances of going out of business.

You must keep an eye on your cash flow.

In my business, we do payroll for our employees and pay our bills twice a month: on the first of the month (FOM) and on the 15th (middle of the month or MOM). We religiously devote those two days to pay our bills and review our finances. We don't address our finances randomly or haphazardly. We never find ourselves saying (as I've heard some business owners utter), "Better spend this weekend catching up on the bills!"

Catch up? Managing the money is one of the most important functions of your entire business! Once you get behind on that, there is no catching up. The entrepreneurs who master the money will master their business.

Small businesses are the backbone of this country and sound money management is critical to their success. Therefore, I cannot stress enough the point we discussed earlier regarding hiring the right team for your business: *If you aren't good at watching the numbers, hire one or more good, full-time, in-office bookkeepers.*

Find Certified Public Accountants (CPAs) who focus on your industry. You wouldn't see one physician to care for your eyes, teeth, heart, the bunion on your foot, and your migraine headaches. You'd seek out specialists for those things. Similarly you want to work with a specialized CPA who knows your industry and can cater to your business. To find specialists in the field of dentistry, my colleagues and I can look to the Academy of Dental CPAs and the Institute of Dental CPAs.

Also be sure to choose a CPA who wants you to be fully informed and clear about your own numbers. Historically, the accepted business model has discouraged transparency. In the entryway of my home hangs a framed copy of Martin Luther's "Ninety-five Theses"—a perfect example of the importance of transparency. Luther wrote the document in 1517 challenging the Catholic Church as the supreme religious authority (as opposed to the Bible), and, specifically, the Church's practice of selling "indulgences" to insure the purchaser against eternal damnation.

Until Luther, a monk, translated the Bible from Greek to German, the people of Germany had to rely on Church leaders to tell them what it contained. Luther made the Bible accessible to Germans, thus exposing the corruption going on among Church leadership.

Luther's work brought transparency to the business practices of the 16th Century Catholic Church. Yet the model still exists in which people rely solely on the "experts" to manage the financial aspects of their business, while the "experts" purposefully keep them in the dark about what is actually going on to better their own bottom line. Many business owners place their trust in the hands of a CPA who can't, or won't, explain their finances in a way they can understand and base sound decisions upon. A good CPA wants you to possess the same level of knowledge and comprehension of your financial reports as she does. If she can't, or won't, answer your questions to your complete satisfaction, find a CPA who will.

Along with a good CPA to ensure you're meeting federal guidelines for your daily accounting activities and accurately calculating your annual tax liability, you need an employee *in-house* to manage and advise you on your finances on a daily basis.

Every business from McDonald's to Subway, from Southwest Airlines to Wal-Mart has software that tracks its numbers. Any manager can go to their computer at any time during the day and see their sales, labor, lab, supplies, marketing, and net income for the hour, day, month, or year.

Knowing the status of your receivables is especially important, because that ties directly into cash flow. A lot of people think that price is the most important variable in cash flow, but I'm going to argue that it is the second most important variable behind your collections policy. We'll explore collections in more detail later, but for now keep in mind that the status of your receivables is a vital number to watch.

DEBT-TO-INCOME RATIO

Now that you have looked at your statement of income, balance sheet and statement of cash flow, you need to know how they affect you and whether you're underwater or safe to keep going. The best way to do this is to calculate your debt-to-income ratio. Divide your monthly payments by your monthly gross revenue (before taxes and deductions) and multiply by 100. The result will give you a pretty solid indication as to how you're holding up. The higher your percentage, the more debt you have. If possible, you want to keep it below 40 percent.

AUDIT REPORTS

Most accounting software has an audit trail. If you don't print and monitor your audit trail report on a regular basis, you need to start now. It doesn't take a genius to make a product at a loss, but you can look like a genius if you can make a product or provide a service at a profit.

There are different kinds of audit reports. Some software programs have an actual audit trail, or you can develop your own audit for your business that double-checks the income posted on a weekly basis.

There are two reasons why you should print and review the audit trail report on a regular basis: because of rampant embezzlement occurring in businesses of every size, and for training purposes. An audit trail is essentially a record of who has done what in the accounting software. It's something you can fall back on when questioning something in the numbers. The obvious reason is to catch any transactions that are being deleted or changed, affecting your collections or production. Reduce your risk of embezzlement by staying on top of your audit trail. The second reason is for training purposes. If a staff member posts incorrectly and doesn't realize the repercussions, you can address the problem promptly.

Let's say you see a huge mistake that no one can account for. You can go in and trace who did what to help find the answer. In my business, typically we can find out what happened by looking at the journal entries, but the audit trail is a handy, reliable backup.

Remember: All mistakes in accounting can be fixed. People make mistakes, and you can easily make mistakes in your entries. You will find them in the reconciliation process and double checks and, when you do, you can fix them. It's as easy as reversing a transaction. You are working with an entry, not with the money that's in the bank account, so there's no need to panic.

EXPENSES TO MONITOR

Here are the critical expenses to watch:

OVERHEAD

We can essentially break down overhead into two categories: overhead you can control and overhead you cannot control. When I talk to other businesspeople, a lot of the overhead they complain about is out of their control; labor, for instance. Most overhead is determined by supply and demand. If the average dental hygienist makes thirty-five dollars an hour in your city, you can't afford to say, "Oh, thirty-five dollars an hour is too high. I need to bring our costs down, so I'm only going to pay my hygienist thirty dollars an hour." Your hygienist will quit and find another place to work that's paying market wages.

You cannot control what the government charges you in taxes, or what the power company charges you for electricity. I live in Phoenix, Arizona, a city powered by a $10 billion nuclear power plant. My electricity payment goes toward keeping that thing running. I can't just call up the electric company and ask them to lower my bill.

So much of your overhead is set by the free market that the only way to really control overhead is to work backwards from that number. For example, if all the dentists in an area pay their hygienists thirty-five dollars an hour, then you need to try to get your hygienist to offer your patient more goods and services so you can bill out more per hour and make your existing overhead more efficient and productive.

The same goes for electricity; you can't control what the local utility is going to charge for electricity, but you can set up your business to "go green" by conserving electricity through everything from insulation to windows to energy-efficient hot water heaters.

In my field, many dentists have joined the Eco Dentistry Association, an organization that offers educational programs, research, and member resources helping dental professionals reduce our environmental impact, cut costs, and attract the growing population of wellness lifestyle patients. Dentists are investing in solar and wind power. Some have gone completely off the grid. It is not only conscientious to go green; it is profitable.

Don't waste your time trying to fight the existing cost of your goods and services set by free enterprise. If goods and services set by the marketplace cost you a dollar per day and you do a dollar a day in sales, your overhead is 100 percent. If you figure out how to increase your revenue to two dollars a day, voila, there's 50 percent overhead—the same percentage maintained by the most successful businesses in the world—from dental practices to Intel. The company with 100 percent overhead and the company with 50 percent overhead are probably paying the same in tax rates, utilities, and employee salaries, but the business that is profitable, expanding, and making *you* a millionaire is the one that succeeds in getting two dollars of revenue out of each dollar of overhead.

Collection	Overhead	Paycheck
$125,000	80%	$25,000
$71,500	65%	$25,000
$50,000	50%	$25,000
$41,667	40%	$25,000

When I think of lowering overhead, I think of getting more revenue from my existing overhead, the cost of which is mostly out of my control. I can only control how to most efficiently use those goods and services.

COMPENSATION

This is the largest expense for any business. In fact, Fortune 500 companies average 50 percent labor expense. In most dental practices, payroll accounts for around 50 percent of total overhead. America has 117 towns with a population of over 100,000 people. And in those towns, labor (including hygienists, receptionists, and assistants), accounts for 25 percent of the cost of a dental practice, while the dentist, on average, accounts for 35 percent. That means that in the 117 towns that have more than 100,000 people, a dental practice is looking at a total labor cost of 60 percent. In the 19,033 towns in America with under 100,000 people (the average being about 5,000 people), the labor cost for hygienists, receptionists, and assistants stands at around 20 percent.

I cannot emphasize enough that when you're starting a small business, opening in one of America's 117 largest cities is a surefire way to have higher overhead. The hidden jewels for small business are America's rural areas. Half of America lives in rural areas. The labor, buildings, and other facilities are much lower in cost. In fact it's not unheard of for a small business to go into a small town where right there on the corner of First Street and Main is a building that's been sitting empty for twenty years, and the city happily sells it for a dollar just to see some new economic activity.

We've seen this in California where some of the greatest startups moved an hour's drive away from Silicon Valley to small towns where, for the same rent they would have to pay in urban areas, they found facilities ten times larger and employees at half the cost. Wouldn't you rather be a big fish in a small pond than a small fish in the ocean? In a small town, the mayor is going to know you by your first name and you're ten times more likely to get a loan from a local bank. There are literally thousands of small towns in America that don't have a single dentist, physician, or electrician. Move to one of those, and you have a monopoly. The professionals who make money right out of college set up their businesses in small-town America.

As we've discussed, it is important to pay your people well to show you value them and maintain customer trust and satisfaction. However, take care not to go overboard, even though it is tempting when times are good. Because what will you do if business slows? You need to be prepared for that. You might need to institute cost-saving measures such as making your employees pay 25 percent of their health insurance premiums, or not matching their 401(k)s. You might even need to let people go to ensure your business stays afloat. This is never fun, but if you know your numbers—if you're actively watching them—you can better prepare yourself and your company when things aren't looking so good.

Remember, the easiest dollar earned is a dollar in expenses saved. Spend more time figuring out what you can save rather than what you can sell.

MARKETING AND ADVERTISING

In good times, you want to market yourself, but in bad times you *really* want to market yourself! Michael Dell's greatest gift to business, in my opinion, was *not* the mass customization of the personal computer when everyone else was mass-producing a one-size-fits-all model. What

Michael Dell really showed the world after the stock market crash in March 2000 was that when the market plummets, you double or triple your marketing efforts.

Dell knew he was losing a lot of his existing business, so what did he do? He hit the airwaves with a new campaign around the slogan: *Dude, you're getting a Dell.* He doubled down on advertising, and his company revenues skyrocketed during a down period in the US economy.

When revenue is down, so many businesses look at advertising and marketing as an unnecessary expense and drop it. That is the kiss of death! When your revenue is down, you need to massively increase your efforts. I know it sounds counterintuitive, but it's a fact.

While both are important, there is a difference between advertising and marketing. Advertising is directed toward bringing new customers in your front door; marketing is designed to keep your existing customers from leaving out your back door. To put it another way, think of advertising as the means of generating the flow of water down the Colorado River into the Hoover Dam reservoir, and marketing as the means of shoring up the dam to keep any water from escaping.

Advertising is broadcasting to everyone in your market whether through radio, television, widely circulated print ads, or other methods that reach a large market including the Internet. Marketing—which also includes customer service, media, and PR—targets your existing customers. You can be a master at attracting new customers, but if you continuously lose customers out your back door, you'll never have a successful business.

The best companies have the highest percent of sales going toward advertising. At my dental office, I have spent no less than 3 percent of revenue on advertising for twenty-five years through good times and bad. During the bad times, however, I have increased it to 5 percent. I've even borrowed money in order to advertise with big campaigns.

During the early years of my practice, I took out ads in the local newspaper to announce the birth of each of my sons. I ran a family-oriented dental practice, and my ads spoke to parents—particularly mothers—who wanted that kind of practice for their own families. I got to show off my beautiful babies to the community, and, as a bonus, attracted more patients to my business.

Advertising is not something you can just stop doing. If you do, good luck. Companies that stop advertising and marketing in down economies always take a larger hit than they would had they gotten their names in front of more and more people.

You also need to be able to determine the best return on investment (ROI) for your marketing dollar. Try new things and track what's giving you the best bang for your marketing buck. Back in the good old days, all it took was an ad in the Yellow Pages and maybe some direct mail pieces to market a dental practice. Today you've got the Internet, search engine optimization (SEO), texting, and social media. Direct mail and the Yellow Pages may or may not work in your market; some dental offices report that neither of those work for them anymore, although this tends to be more the case in urban markets. In rural markets, Yellow Pages advertising and direct mail are still effective.

The key is to track *everything!*

A little note about SEO. I am not an SEO specialist, but I'm here to tell you that you need to find one! When I got out of school twenty-five years ago, innovations such as smart phones, digital books (such as Kindle and Nook), and Google didn't exist. I live and work in the fifth largest city in America where there are 3,500 other practicing dentists. *I need an SEO specialist.* I work extremely closely with one whose advice and expertise are invaluable to my business and me. I've learned that the clear leader in Internet search engines is Google, that Google owns YouTube, and that by updating your website weekly or monthly with a one-minute YouTube video explaining your newest product, service, or special, you help bump your website to the top of Google searches. The same goes for Google+.

Google wants to see activity on your website, because its entire business is to serve up the best websites for its customers' searches. If Google always finds what its customers are looking for, it will continue to be a $20 billion a year giant.

So say you're a plumber and there are five websites for plumbers in your town, four of which were built three years ago and nothing's been updated on any of them since. But Google sees your website is always being updated with fresh content and that people are reading well beyond your home page. That does wonders for your website's SEO and, therefore, your business.

The definition of an entrepreneur is someone who continually moves their money and assets from lower to higher rates of return. So, if grandma only has one $5,000 CD to her name and she moves it from one bank paying 2 percent interest to a bank that pays 3 percent interest, grandma is an entrepreneur! If your advertising budget is $1,000 per month, then as an entrepreneur, your job is to move those dollars from less cost effective methods—which in my case were the Yellow Page ads—to more cost effective options such as digital Internet marketing.

Bottom line, tracking is everything when it comes to advertising. You want to attract the greatest number of new customers for the least amount of money.

What I see too often—whether among plumbers, restaurateurs, or dentists—are business owners who spend all their time making something. Again, the people who focus more on the money—on watching the numbers—than they do on making their product are infinitely more successful. You'll be a lot better off having a well-run business focusing on the numbers with an average product than you will having an outstanding product with no one watching the numbers.

Remember: *Watching the numbers is more important than making your product.* So if you haven't already, go run your reports. Find out what your numbers are. And if the numbers aren't where you want them to be, find ways to improve them! Maybe you can begin including new procedures, goods, or services in your business or figure out better ways to market to your customers.

ACTION POINTS

- Make sure you and your team know the numbers. The business-person who knows the score is infinitely more successful than the businessperson who does not. You should know the score and so should your team!

- Prepare a statement of income that shows your revenue, expenses (fixed and variable) and net profit. Your net profit is your bottom line. Without a net profit, you're finished. End of story.

- Prepare a balance sheet that shows your assets (current and fixed), liabilities (current and long term), and equity.

- Prepare a statement of cash flow.

- Establish and maintain a $10,000 floor in your business checking account.

- Establish a line of credit. If the bank turns down your application, use the opportunity to listen to the reasons why, and then take the necessary measures to enable your business to qualify.

- Determine your debt to income ratio.

- Conduct regular audit reports.

- Monitor your overhead, compensation, marketing, and advertising.

- Figure out ways to make your existing overhead more efficient and profitable.

- When the economy is up, advertise. When the economy is down, advertise even more! Track your marketing. Make sure you're getting the best bang for your buck!

- Use a CPA who specializes in your industry. If you're a plumber, do not use a CPA who only has one other plumber on his or her roster. Use a CPA who works with dozens of other plumbers.

If you can't explain it simply,
you don't understand it well enough.

—*Albert Einstein*

Create a Budget

Now that you know what your numbers are, you have to be able to use them as a measurement of your business. The way you do that is to create a budget.

BENCHMARKING

Before you can get started on developing your business's budget, you should figure out the lay of the land and how you compare to others in your particular field. You should know the benchmarks in your industry regarding expenditures for labor, supplies, utilities, advertising, facility expenses, etc. Compare your percentages to the industry benchmark and evaluate where you are (with respect to net income) to see whether you are meeting your goals.

Remember, most industries have been around for centuries. You're not the first construction company, plumber, or restaurateur on the planet. I like to look at the statement of income, the statement of cash flow, and balance sheet information of publicly traded companies; all of that information is available and pretty easy to grab off of the Internet. But for those of us who don't have any competition in the public market, information is available through resourceful websites such as www.bizminer.com. Bizminer compiles information from hundreds of companies and publishes benchmarking averages for you to look at and study—for a nominal fee, of course.

Every businessperson needs to have a LinkedIn account. If you do a search for people in your industry, you'll be surprised at how much information they will share with you. Twenty percent of all the best plumbers are listed on LinkedIn. Whatever your business, take the time to network; send your competitors an email to ask what information they are willing to share with you.

Why do you want to benchmark? The answer is simple: when you know what the average companies in your industry are doing, you have a basis upon which to build your budget (how much you should be spending and on what), and to create your financial goals.

BUILD A BUDGET

Many businesses operate under the formula, *cost + profit = price*. If each tomato costs one dollar to produce, and the producers want a one-dollar profit, then they set the price of each tomato at two dollars.

This is a formula for failure.

What if they can't sell any tomatoes at two dollars? They end up going out of business.

In business, you set the price *first*. Determine the price at which your product will sell, subtract your profit, and now you have a *budget*.

Price – profit = budget.

So if I sell the tomatoes in the market for one dollar and I make a 10 percent profit margin, I have a budget of ninety cents. If I can't bring my tomatoes to market for ninety cents, then I don't have a business, because tomatoes are selling for one dollar.

The goal is to stay within the parameters of the benchmark percentages when you build a budget.

Price is a very important variable in business. This is where the term *price elasticity* comes from. Price has a very elastic effect on demand. The higher the price, the less you will sell; the lower the price, the more you will sell. In fact some business people consider "price" as marketing. Want to sell a lot more furniture (like IKEA) or plane tickets (like Southwest Airlines)? Just lower your price! That low price could be the best marketing you've ever had! The low prices Southwest Airlines can offer by having a low-cost structure is that company's best marketing tool. Of course they spend money on television commercials and billboards touting their low prices, but you know what lets most people know about Southwest Airlines? Word-of-mouth referrals from happy customers!

You need to determine the price of your product and you need to make a profit. You cannot build a high-quality Mercedes-Benz and sell it for the price of a Chevrolet or you will go bankrupt.

We see this in dentistry all the time. After signing up for an insurance plan that gives the dentist the price schedule, the dentist should subtract the profit she needs to maintain a 50 to 65 percent overhead, and then arrive at a budget to do the dentistry. But this isn't what the dentist generally does. The dentist doesn't care what the budget is for the dentistry. The dentist has all these ideas that dental restorations should be all tooth colored or made of solid gold or made by the best, most expensive dental labs in America. She tells herself and others that she only wants to do dentistry on her patients the way she would want in her own mouth. Trust me; I understand the idea of dentistry—of any profession—as a sacred calling.

But it makes no more sense for a dentist to say, "I will only do dentistry on all my patients the way I'd want it done in my own mouth," than it would for a car salesperson to say, "I will only sell my customers a car that I would buy for myself, and I would only drive a

Mercedes-Benz." Not every driver puts the same value on an expensive car like that.

I have seven fillings in my mouth and they're all gold. Why? Because I highly value the dentistry in my own mouth. Gold is awesome. You can't break it. It lasts forever. But not everyone has the money to pay for a gold filling. Some people need a lower cost option and simply want you to fix their tooth professionally, but at the lowest cost possible.

When it comes to price elasticity, the important thing to remember is that there will always be a low-volume, high-cost market—for Mercedes, for example—and there will always be a much larger, high-volume, low-cost market—such as for Chevys.

Again, benchmarking enables you to see what others in your industry are doing so you have a basis for determining consumer demand in your market and the price points for your products and services.

There's not a single publicly traded company on the Standard & Poor's 500 index that doesn't have its budget in place for the entire year at least a month before the year begins. Every successful business starts with a budget. Create a budget *at the start of your business* and *put it in writing*. Overlook that step and there's no point in starting a business at all.

Remember, work like no man has for a decade and you can reap like no man has for the rest of your life.

ACTION POINTS

- Build your budget.

- Know your benchmarks. If you don't have any personal information to go by, research your industry and find out the average revenue and costs associated with your business. This is key to figuring out whether or not you're on the right track.

- Determine the difference between what you've budgeted and what you actually paid out. Doing this helps you gauge where you can make adjustments to either increase your revenue or lower your costs.

- When in doubt, consult the pros! There are a variety of resources you can consult to create a budget that works for you.

A budget tells us what we can't afford,
but it doesn't keep us from buying it.

—William Feather

Make Your Numbers
Work for You

Once you know what your numbers are, you can use them to maximize your business.

Let's go back to the DuPont Formula we discussed in Section II. In the first two parts of this equation, profit margin is determined by net income divided by the dollar amount of sales, and the return on assets (ROA) by the dollar amount of sales divided by the value of assets.

As we discussed, by introducing the buffet, Dan Carney increased the number of customers he could serve at a Pizza Hut at any given time, thus increasing his profit margin and his return on assets.

This leads us to the third part of the formula: leverage. If you buy a business by putting down only 10 percent of the purchase price and borrowing the rest, you are leveraged ten-fold. This largely determines your return on equity, which is profit margin × turnover × equity.

The DuPont Formula:

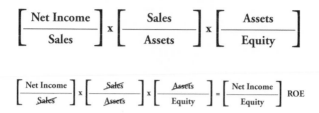

Return On Equity

Why should you leverage your business? The simple answer is that there is only so much a person can do independently by working. Consider this: If you earned $15 per hour working twelve hours per day, seven days per week, 365 days per year for 2,000 years, you still would not earn $1 billion. There are only three ways to become a billionaire. The first is to inherit from a billionaire. The second is to marry a billionaire. The third is to borrow other people's money (OPM) and buy or build something that pays back the billion dollars. This is called *leverage*.

Your accounting numbers also help you manage supply and demand.

The most successful restaurants are the ones that have mastered supply and demand. McDonald's continually adjusts supply to increasing demand. When I opened up my dental office in 1987, Ahwatukee had one McDonald's. Twenty-five years later, Ahwatukee has three McDonald's.

Consider banks. When banks build their drive-through lanes, they know that in a 168-hour week, they may only need one lane for much of that time. But when payday comes on Friday, customers will flock to their ATMs. So they construct three drive-through lanes to match capacity to the flow of the demand.

Go into a Barnes & Noble bookstore, and often you might find only one employee checking people out. Yet because the company knows its demand comes in waves, there is the capacity for eight checkout registers. At times of high demand—say, when a movie lets out at the theater next door—all eight registers will be humming. The company has tracked the numbers and set up its stores to match capacity with the flow of customers.

In a nutshell, you don't match your capacity and infrastructure to your total demand. That only works on an assembly line where a Ford truck is coming down the line and you only make so many trucks per hour. You match your capacity and infrastructure to the *flow* of your demand. Every millionaire businessperson I know has excess capacity and infrastructure to match the flow of demand. If you are a retail outlet in a mall, and you know you are going to sell 40 percent of your year's merchandise over the Christmas holidays, you keep excess inventory in a warehouse ready to meet that demand. You don't plan your inventory to sell X units per day, because you don't sell X units per day.

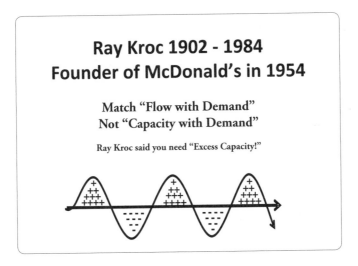

Ray Kroc 1902 - 1984
Founder of McDonald's in 1954

Match "Flow with Demand"
Not "Capacity with Demand"

Ray Kroc said you need "Excess Capacity!"

Again, match your capacity and infrastructure to the flow of your demand—not to the total demand.

I explained this to my four boys when they were little using a model of a go-kart. I'd tell my boys, "The go-kart represents your business and the racetrack represents the flow of customers through your business. When customers start stacking up in front of your go-kart, you only have two options because you only have two pedals. You can (A) slow down (or brake) by raising your price; that way you'll get the maximum amount of money from the people who want and value your product or service the most.

Brake

1) Raise
Your
Prices

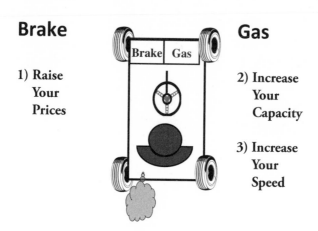

Gas

2) Increase
Your
Capacity

3) Increase
Your
Speed

"Your other option is to (B) punch the gas pedal to create more capacity. A restaurant for example might add more tables to increase the number of customers it can serve at any one time."

Let me show you an example of a dental office. Let's say a customer walks into your office one day and asks for a cleaning. Given your schedule, you have to tell that person you don't have an opening. You have two options for creating that opening in the future.

Say the hygienist you currently employ charges $70 for a cleaning (not counting the X-rays and the exam). If that hygienist sees eight people in an eight-hour day, she collects $560 using 100 percent of her capacity. Any patient waiting in the lobby creates an instant bottleneck. By simply raising the price to $80, one patient may decide to leave you, but that's ok, because you have another patient at the front door eager to come in for the additional $10. You still get your $560 from seven patients at the higher price while using only 87.5% of your capacity. Now that person standing at the front door can come in and pay you an additional $80. You just increased capacity simply by raising your price.

You also can increase your capacity by increasing your speed and efficiency, such as adding new equipment to take the place of older, slower methods—the way Dan Carney did when he switched from menus to a buffet in his Pizza Hut restaurants. When I got out of dental school, we did root canals by hand; now we have automated root canal machines that automatically file out the tooth. We also have CAD/CAM machines that automatically mill out a crown, in house, and in the same patient appointment.

Essentially, you do what every assembly line in America has done for the last century: incrementally improve thousands of little things so that the assembly line goes a little bit faster every month.

Another way to increase your capacity is to add personnel.

In a dental office, a hygienist who cleans teeth can clean eight hours a day, five days a week; that's forty hours a week. Assuming there's no gum disease, the average person gets their teeth cleaned twice a year for an hour. Forty hours a week times fifty weeks a year equals 2,000 hours. That means your hygienist can only clean the teeth of about 1,000 people twice a year. Yet while the average dental office in America has 5,000 charts, most do not have a single full-time hygienist working forty hours a week. The average dental office, at best, has one hygienist working four days a week. That's a good way to lose patients.

Scheduling . . . Hygiene

Weeks per year	X	Hours per week	X	No. of Hygienists	÷	6 month recall	=	Hygiene Capacity (no. patients)
50		40		1		2		1000
50		32		2		2		1600

Source: A Consumerist's Road Map
By Howard Farran DDS, MBA, MAGD, Copyright 1997

Depending on the supply and demand of the local demographics, or how much money is committed to advertising and marketing, let's look at how long it takes for a dental practice to get to one thousand patients, facilitating the need for a full-time hygienist. If you are only getting ten new patients a month, it will take you one hundred months to reach one thousand patients. Twenty new patients a month would take fifty months. Thirty new patients would take thirty months; forty would take twenty-five months. With one hundred new patients a month, you'd have a full-time hygienist in ten months.

The top 20 percent of dentists in America need to have an associate dentist. There are 168 hours in a week. The fixed cost of a dental office—land, building, equipment, computers, insurance, software—is paid for and it's literally only open 25 percent of the week. Yet most dentists have an excuse for not bringing on an associate. I've heard dentists claim they can't find an associate willing to work extended hours in their little town.

Really? The United States military employs 5,000 dentists and puts them in scary places like Iraq, Afghanistan, the 38th Parallel, North Korea, or on an aircraft carrier for six months at a time, yet these dentists can't find a dentist for their quiet, rural offices? If they were to look at their numbers, they could see the benefit of an associate to their bottom line.

Whether you have a dental practice, a restaurant, or a pool cleaning service, it is crucial to track all your numbers to manage your supply and demand.

So stay focused on the numbers. Your bottom line will thank you.

ACTION POINTS

- Use your numbers to determine the flow of your supply and demand.
- Make any necessary adjustments to your capacity (e.g. increase your price, add capacity to your physical space, add personnel, increase your speed and efficiency with new technology) to match your capacity to the flow of demand.

What gets measured gets managed.

—Peter Drucker

Collections

Collecting money at the time of sale is the most important insurance policy you can have in order to stay in business. You can't give someone $1,000 worth of goods and services and get paid ninety days later, because you need ninety days worth of cash to maintain your operations—to pay for labor, supplies, rent, mortgage, equipment, computers, insurance, and software—while you're waiting to get paid. So if your business does $100,000 a month in sales, you effectively need $300,000 in savings because you're getting paid three months behind.

The geniuses at business reverse this strategy; they collect all of their money at the time of sale and then they pay all of *their* bills three months down the line—effectively getting a $300,000 loan at zero percent interest.

This is why selling traveler's checks was one of the most profitable businesses in America for a century. Before going on vacation, consumers bought travelers checks that weren't cashed for days, weeks, maybe even months. That traveler's check company basically sat on a mountain of free cash.

American business magnate Warren Buffett loves insurance for that very reason. While consumers pay their regular insurance premiums to the companies he owns, such as Geico, those claims won't be made for a lot longer. So along with the profit he has made in previous years, he can invest money paid to him today that won't be paid out until later. So the collection policy is absolutely one of the most important variables in business.

Now that you have a system for reviewing your key numbers, you need to be aware of two things that can affect your business. Nobody (especially professionals) likes to talk about collections or embezzlement, but these two things can destroy your business.

WATCH YOUR RECEIVABLES

At one of my recent seminars, I was asked, "What do you do when you practice in a town of five thousand people and one of your patients hasn't paid you for six months?"

This is one of those questions I hate to answer because no one wins in this scenario. It is one of the lousiest situations in the history of lousy situations.

Reluctantly, I responded to the dentist that he had a couple of options, neither of them good. As the dentist, you can turn Mr. Jones over to collections, which will likely ruin his credit, which means every time you run into Mr. Jones at the bank or the grocery store, you each will feel major pangs of guilt—or worse. Or, you can write off Mr. Jones' bill, but that only suggests to Mr. Jones that the dental work he received might not have been quality, because you aren't valuing it.

Because of Mr. Jones' unwillingness to pay, it's a lose-lose proposition no matter how you slice it. Either you write it off and he gets away with hundreds or thousands of dollars in dentistry, or you unleash the hounds and destroy Mr. Jones' credit and your reputation around town as a "nice guy."

Faced with either option, my suggestion to the gentleman asking the question was to write a list of the pros and cons of going after

Mr. Jones' money and a second list of the pros and cons of writing off Mr. Jones' treatment. The list with the fewer consequences—or with the consequences the doctor could best live with—would be the one to win out. Obviously, the consequences of your decision tend to be greater in a rural community—where more people know each other—than in a larger community. But like I said, it's a lousy situation no matter what. At most dental practices I see, the patient comes in with a problem, the doctor treats it and then spends the rest of her time tracking down the money owed to her.

But you can avoid it!

Consider fast-food restaurants. Does McDonald's have collection problems? No! And why?

1. They take your order.
2. They take your money.
3. They give you what you ordered

No teenager behind the counter at McDonald's has a problem asking for and collecting money from the customers, because of one simple policy: no food unless you've paid for it.

Why not make all of your customers read and sign a collections policy that states they have to pay their share *up front*, instead of this ridiculous backward way so many businesses operate under—many of them failing as a result?

So many dental practices wait for insurance to pay out before they bill the patient—and their collections are a nightmare. My patients understand that their portion is due on the day of treatment, and we can proudly say that our collections percentage is upward of 99 percent. Any patient who throws a fit about our policy wouldn't have paid us anyway.

When a dentist performs dentistry on a customer who hasn't paid up front, the customer now has an economic incentive *not* to pay the dentist. Customers can begin thinking up reasons to rationalize not paying at all.

I know competent, highly professional dentists who've encountered patients who threaten to report them to the Better Business Bureau for doing shoddy work.

As a professional, such a blatantly dishonest encounter puts a knot in your stomach as you start having nightmares about facing more problems from this yahoo. So rather than dealing with a potentially bigger mess, you write it off.

But here's the thing; these people know that what they are doing is wrong. That's why they go to such lengths to justify in their own minds that you are not a good dentist, you are not a nice guy, and your dental office is no good. They'll never come back to the practice ever again. You've not only lost your money, but a patient—perhaps more than one patient if that person is associated with other people connected to your practice.

It's a disaster! And all because the dental practice does not have a firm collections policy.

Let me make this real simple. If your business sells something for three dollars and it costs two dollars in overhead to make it, then your profit is one dollar. If you don't get paid your three dollars, you still spent two dollars making it, so that means the next two dollars of profit is going to pay for overhead and expenses that went into the product you should have sold for three dollars.

If a business has a 20 percent profit margin and 10 percent of its customers don't pay, half of your overhead is the result of your collection policy.

There's another consequence dentists often fail to consider. While they spent an hour of their time doing Mr. Won't-Pay's crown, another patient, Mr. Pays, who has been with the dental practice for ten years suffered a broken tooth and needed to come in (and would happily have paid for everything on a credit card). However, since the dentist was so busy doing free dentistry on Mr. Won't-Pay, Mr. Pays couldn't be fit into the schedule. Now the dentist is not only out the $1,000 from Mr. Won't-Pay, he's out the $1,000 he could have collected from

Mr. Pays. That's a two-thousand-dollar difference on the statement of cash flow!

If you work in retail, you are fortunate in that you get the cash or credit up front, and nobody's walking out of your store with any new item unless they've purchased it first. In my opinion, the same standard should apply in every industry. A customer should pay for what they want up front rather than leave you to send a bill that they may or may not pay in the end.

Get a collections policy in place and adhere to it. Once you start consistently collecting what your customers owe you at the time of sale, most of your collections headaches will disappear. You are not a bank! Stop extending credit to someone you know nothing about.

In September of 2012, a 44-year-old chemist named Jayesh Prajapati—a man who emigrated from India to Canada and went to work as a gas station attendant to support his family—was slain as he tried to stop a gas-and-dash motorist from stealing $112 worth of gasoline. Measures in place to force all gas pumpers to pay up front would literally have saved a man's life.

I cannot stress enough: get paid for your goods and/or services *up front*. Get cash. Get a credit card. Outsource to a finance company. However you do it, get paid at the time of sale.

ACTION POINTS

- Develop a collection policy!
- Inform your customers of your in-house policy and give it to them in writing.
- Include your policy in your company handbook.

Words pay no debts.

—William Shakespeare

Prevent Embezzlement

"I can't believe this happened to me."

"I should have paid more attention to my own books."

"She worked for me for fifteen years. I trusted her."

"I should have made my own deposits."

These distressing quotes are a minute representation of the numerous stories I've heard from owners who have experienced employees embezzling money from their business. I have been consulting for twenty-five years in dentistry, and I have many close friends in the consulting business. We all universally agree on one thing: Walk into any dental office in America and check for embezzlement and you will find it 50 percent of the time. My friends who consult in other small businesses in America report the same percentage.

So what does this mean? If you own a small business, there's a 50/50 chance you're being embezzled from today. There is no foolproof system for protecting against embezzlement, but removing the opportunities will dramatically reduce your chances of it happening to you. Unfortunately, and all too commonly, small businesses fail to take the steps to protect themselves from embezzlement until after the crime has been committed.

One day a colleague approached me with a story about how his front-office employee had embezzled money from him *and* his partner before she was caught. This front-office employee deposited insurance checks into her own accounts located at several different banks. She had a stamp made with her name on it to enable her to add her name to the check. The banks where the deposits were made took the checks without question; since they saw her so often, they assumed there was no problem. She posted the insurance checks to the patients' accounts in the practice management software. Patients never received statements and the outstanding insurance report did not reflect a problem. Since she only went to the bank once or twice each week, there was no daily deposit slip to match up to a day sheet. The dentists failed to request any paperwork from her on a daily basis, eliminating any checks and balances for collections.

This woman was caught only after the second dentist started questioning the low deposits. During the investigation, the deposits from the first dentist showed up and the dentist was notified. Up to that point, the dentist was unaware that any money had been stolen from her. By then, this front office employee had left the dentists' office for reasons other than embezzlement. She currently faces felony charges and the total amount stolen from both doctors is still under investigation.

Embezzlement happens all the time throughout the business world. From dental offices, as in the story above, to the corner gas station with the teenage employee giving his friends free Slurpees and nachos, to billion dollar companies such as Enron and its upper management's creatively planned accounting loopholes. No matter how thoroughly protected you think your business is, it can happen to you.

I want to help keep you from becoming a victim.

The key to preventing embezzlement in your business lies in improving hiring protocols, watching for the warning signs, and insisting on high ethical standards among your staff. In addition, you must establish internal controls, implement strong internal systems and do regular safeguard checks.

IMPROVE YOUR HIRING PROTOCOLS

Do you perform credit checks on new employees? Do you perform background checks on prospective employees? The number-one indicator of future behavior is past behavior. If someone applying to work for you has a record of criminal behavior, chances are good you'll be the next victim.

Do you have a drug-free workplace policy in place and do you conduct drug testing? The sad truth is that desperate people often do desperate things. At a dental practice, an addict will steal both money *and* drugs. I've seen it happen too many times.

You must take measures to ensure you are hiring trustworthy, ethical people.

WATCH FOR THE WARNING SIGNS

There are signs to look for even among the most reliable staff. Warning signs among employees include asking for cash advances, living beyond their means, wanting to work after hours, barring others from their work area, unwillingness to teach others the computer software, eagerness to go to the bank or get the mail, and personal problems (such as gambling, marital issues, and drug or other addictions).

Another red flag is resistance to take earned time off. When you have an employee who doesn't want to take time off, doesn't want to delegate, doesn't want anyone to know his job—he's waving red flags right in your face. He knows that anyone knowledgeable enough to replace him will discover the embezzlement.

Remember the Mack Truck test? My business is set up so that if someone on my team is run over by a Mac Truck and killed, everything keeps moving along as though nothing happened. This not only ensures my business runs smoothly under any circumstance, it prevents any one employee from concealing wrongful behavior.

There's no guarantee that someone who has been with you for fifteen or twenty years won't up and start stealing from you. Statistically, those experiencing a great deal of drama—whether due to a financial crisis, substance abuse, or family problems—are more likely to embezzle from your company. In my career in dentistry, I've encountered colleagues whose spouse embezzled the money in preparation for filing for divorce.

ESTABLISH INTERNAL CONTROLS, STRONG INTERNAL SYSTEMS, AND REGULAR SAFEGUARD CHECKS

Does your business have systems or internal controls in place to prevent embezzlement? Do you and your employees follow a system of checks and balances?

Internal controls involve a process that occurs each month to make sure the risks are properly managed. The first step is to meet with your staff and involve them in the entire process. Review the daily and monthly cash and accounting practices that take place in your business, and then put written policies and procedures in place that outline each person's responsibilities going forward.

The second step is to assign the financial duties in your business to more than one employee. The person who sorts through the mail, opens payments from customers and enters them in your ledger—or the person who posts payments to their accounts and rings up sales on the cash register—should not be the same person who performs your daily deposit. Internal controls require separate cash handling duties and someone to verify all cash receipts collected. Once the daily deposit is made, someone else needs to reconcile the banking deposit with the daily report from your accounting software. This daily review is critical to the internal control process.

On a monthly basis, you need to reconcile your total deposits for the month from your accounting software with your total collections report that is generated from your business software.

The staff member(s) performing your accounting activities should be your biggest cheerleaders for these internal controls. These controls ensure that their actions—if and when questioned/audited—will always prove to be entirely by the book!

Finally, don't assume your reports are being printed and worked on regularly. Remember: Your audit trail report is invaluable in catching anything that might be suspect.

The key to preventing embezzlement is to make sure it could only happen if two people needed to be in on it. Internal systems—such as separating receivables from payables and assigning two different people to work on them—provide financial checks and balances in your company. It's conceivable you might accidentally hire someone willing to steal from you. It's extremely unlikely, however, that person will succeed in convincing someone else to go in on it. Chances are, even if they were to ask, the other employee would run to you and say, "Hey, you won't believe what so-and-so just asked me to do!"

Just a few final thoughts:

Be open with your staff about your concern regarding embezzlement. Ask the staff, "Are we doing everything we can to make sure nobody's embezzling from inside our company? We need to make sure everyone is on board with this!" Open discussion is a huge deterrent.

My employees know my company bank statements are sent to my home. I personally open the bank statements and review all activity including all check copies. That'll scare any embezzler away.

Aside from preventing embezzlement, there is another benefit to establishing checks and balances in your company: The more people looking at the numbers, the greater the chance someone is going to see ways to lower your cost. You simply can't go wrong by having more than one mind studying and observing your numbers.

ACTION POINTS

- Be transparent about embezzlement with your entire staff.
- Do background checks on all potential new hires.
- Establish internal controls, systems, and checks for you and your staff. Make sure that more than one person is handling the bookkeeping to ensure double-checks.

- Watch for the warning signs. Monitor the performance of your employees and consider performing random drug tests if you notice any unusual behavior.
- Conduct regular audit reports.
- Partner with a CPA.

With all the money my uncle embezzled over the years, it's no surprise he lives in a gated community. But what is amazing, however, is that he somehow managed to get his own cell.

—Jarod Kintz (It Occurred to Me)

22

Focus on Your Core Business

The companies that blow away the competition always reinvest in their core business. If you're not moving faster, more efficiently and offering your goods and services at higher quality but lower cost, you're just spinning your wheels along with everyone else.

When they make a little money and their business is running efficiently, many people decide to take their extra cash and invest outside their business. This almost always is a huge mistake. Talk to your friends and colleagues about their investments in real estate, restaurants, bars, or other small businesses and you will see that almost without exception, these other investments have lost money.

Taking care of the money is all about making the tough decisions, and one of the toughest decisions you have to make is whether or not to reinvest money in your business—rather than in a hobby or your buddy's great new idea.

I recently ate dinner at a Chipotle Mexican Grill. Started by Steve Ellis in 1993 in Denver, Colorado, Chipotle grew at a slow and steady pace until 1998 when McDonald's bought a minority share and then a majority share one year later. By 2003, with McDonald's financial backing, Chipotle expanded to three hundred locations. Then in 2006, McDonald's divested from Chipotle, Boston Market, and other non-core business restaurants.

Why? Why would McDonald's offload these properties? Chipotle is a wildly popular food chain, as is Boston Market.

Answer: The same reason Target sold off Mervyn's in 2004. The same reason Ford Motor Company sold off its Aston Martin division.

Companies like McDonald's, Ford, and Target figured out *the best possible return on investment comes from strict focus on their core business.* McDonald's has some of the toughest competition out there with Burger King, Wendy's, In-N-Out Burger, Sonic, and dozens of other fast food entities nipping at its heels. McDonald's has a major war on its hands and, realizing this, looked inward and decided it wasn't in the company's best interest to spend time trying to master burritos and rotisserie chicken on the side.

The exemplary employees working at its Mervyn's subsidiary did nothing to help Target in its struggle to compete against the giant Wal-Mart. Besides, Mervyn's faced off against Kohl's, Sears, J.C. Penney, and about a dozen other chains that were soundly beating it at its own game. So Target brought all of its Mervyn's superstars back to the mother ship and offloaded the weak department store chain.

The same goes for Ford. Consultants told the carmaker that its best people were working on Aston Martins—a luxury line that caters to a miniscule market and makes little profit. Ford was convinced that it needed to spin off Aston Martin, and move those engineers over to design Lincolns and Mercurys where they could sell ten times the number of its higher-end vehicles.

In selling off these secondary properties, McDonald's, Target, and Ford were able to retool and bring the focus back to what made them exceptional in the first place.

For more than twenty years, I've met dentists from all over the world who are trying to make money on the side. These are dentists who average about $500,000 in collections and take home a little less than $200,000 each year. They have it in their heads that they can make more money and achieve amazing success if they invest some of their time and money in some other venture.

I know hundreds of dentists who collect $1.5 million a year in their practices alone, and believe they can do the same in real estate competing against people who have been working in real estate eight hours a day for twenty years.

One dentist decided to become a part-time cattle farmer. Think about that for a second. There are third-generation cattle farmers out there with a thousand head of cattle and who have thought only about cattle every single day of their lives for decades. Our dentist probably thought about it for a full twenty minutes and had zero experience, yet still believed it to be a promising and lucrative venture.

Please. I think these kinds of distractions are ridiculous. If you're a dentist, be a dentist. If you're a real estate developer, be a real estate developer. Don't try to be a dentist AND a real estate developer.

Stick with what you know! Focus on your core business!

You want to make more money? That's great! Why not invest in your own business? See what your peers are doing to increase revenue, productivity, and the "wow" factor for their customers. Look into new technologies that will improve the way you do business, and when you're done doing that, go get trained in them! Then, when you're proficient in these new technologies, invest 3 percent of your collections in the form of advertising to new customers and marketing to existing customers. A little time, investment, and marketing of technologies that will improve your business makes a lot more sense than renting out or buying another property, hiring a wait staff and cooks, learning the restaurant business in five minutes, and hoping someone comes in to order your daily special. Most likely you'll end up eating crow.

As we've discussed, the value of technology is the ability to make your workforce—always your largest expense category—more efficient and productive. And that can only make your business more profitable.

If you have the money to invest, and you are still renting your business space, upgrade the location of your business. Again, buy your own property. Invest in a location easily seen by passersby. My practice, Today's Dental, averages about one walk-in a day just because people *see it*.

Focus on your core competency. Learn how to do more of what you are already good at and to do it better. I implore my fellow dentists to invest in continuing education. Check out orthodontic classes. Learn about sleep medicine and how to place implants. Invest in new technologies and get trained on them. Make it a goal to be the best businesspeople they can be by investing in their professional development and their practice. Then later on, when they're grossing more than $1.5 million a year and they want to branch out and make more money, instead of opening up *Dr. Smith's Good Eats*, they might actually consider opening up another dental practice.

You need to deploy some capital and do some serious investing in your business. I have written to dentists about investing in new technologies until my fingers bled. Again, it all comes down to three things:

Earn. Save. Reinvest.

Every time you eat out for $100, that money could have purchased $100 worth of Internet ads on Google or Facebook. My dental practice runs advertising on Google and Facebook and they cost us about a dollar a click. I would rather have a hundred clicks to my dental office's website than any fancy dinner. Dental practices need higher patient flow, which equals more cash flow. The smaller your market, the more effective your ads will be. I live in an area of Phoenix, Arizona called "Ahwatukee," and there are 3,600 people on Facebook that cite Ahwatukee in their profile. Every time those 3,600 people log onto Facebook, they might see my ad. A greater percentage of the activity on Facebook comes from women, and women make about 90 percent of all dental appointments.

I'd rather eat at home and put my dining out money toward attracting new clients to my business. If you truly want to invest in something other than your business, take that $100 you would have spent at the restaurant and put it toward serving people in your community, or in other parts of the world, who need your help.

Which brings us to our last chapter and the true goal of success, which resides a place *beyond* the numbers . . .

ACTION POINTS

- Focus on your core business.

- Strive to own your business's property.

- Location. Location. Location! Pick a visible real estate spot if you are in the Business to Consumer (B to C) sector, in which business is conducted between a business and consumers. This is not as important if you are in the Business to Business (B to B) sector, in which commerce is conducted between two or more businesses.

- Determine where you can reinvest in your business to increase your profits, be it hiring more salespeople or investing in new technologies to allow your company to work faster, cheaper, higher in quality, and lower in cost.

You have to have your heart in the business
and the business in your heart.

—Thomas J. Watson

You must not only aim right,
but draw the bow with all your might.

—Henry David Thoreau

23

Beyond the Numbers

You must watch your numbers to succeed in business. However, once your numbers are in order, it's important to realize that to achieve true success, you must look *beyond* the numbers.

In August 2012, I had the opportunity to visit Sweden. It's such a lovely country and the people are so friendly. They're enormously proud of their country's involvement in the global market—from Ericsson to Volvo to Atlas Copco—but the one company that impresses them the most is, as you might guess, IKEA. While I was in Sweden meeting new friends and colleagues, I asked about IKEA founder Ingvar Kamprad.

I knew virtually nothing about the guy except that he had a passion for providing the world with durable, inexpensive furniture. The first thing out of nearly everyone's mouth was some version of, "Mr. Kamprad is one of the world's richest men, but have you seen his house?"

Go ahead; Google "Ingvar Kamprad house" and take a look for yourself. One of the world's richest men—a man worth billions and billions of dollars—lives in a quaint, little bungalow filled with IKEA furniture (naturally). Nobody in Sweden can comprehend that this guy lives so modestly.

It is my opinion that the other millionaires and billionaires of the world—along with people who are dangerously overextending themselves—would do well to try living by Kamprad's modest example. Every single dentist I know lives in a much nicer house than the founder of IKEA.

Warren Buffett shares a similar lifestyle. When I was working on my undergrad at Creighton University in Omaha, Nebraska, I had the opportunity to drive past Buffett's house a couple of times. I was shocked that a man worth as much as Warren Buffett lived in such a modest dwelling. Granted, later in life Buffet purchased his own private jet because he didn't want to deal with public transportation anymore, but he named it *The Indefensible* because he felt there was no way to defend spending what he did on that plane. Yet many people who own private jets barely have a fraction of Warren Buffett's money.

Here's the thing, dear reader; if money is your main goal in life, if that's all you want, you're not only missing out big time, it's also very likely you'll fail to get it. Successful people seek a passion and a purpose in life and, when they find it, the money comes. You may have heard the adage, "Do what you love and the money will follow." I'm here to tell you that it's true!

Successful people live with perpetual intellectual curiosity. Kamprad simply wanted to make low cost furniture. He spent all his time just trying to figure out how to make a durable, good-looking chair as inexpensively as possible, so that he could pass the savings on to his customers.

Thomas Edison was so passionate about his work, he made 10,000 failed attempts before creating the light bulb. He kept at it until he figured it out!

Yet how many people do you know like Mr. Owl from that Tootsie Pop commercial who—when the boy asks how many licks it takes to get to the Tootsie Roll center of a Tootsie Pop—licks the thing three times before biting it off for want of instant gratification?

When it comes to money, the bottom line is this: If you own your own business, live within your means and you will be able to keep following your passion and your purpose for the benefit of your customers.

REEXAMINE YOUR RETIREMENT

After one of my recent lectures, I was shooting the breeze with a few doctors when we got on the topic of retiring in a down economy. One of the docs said, "Y'know guys, I went to a funeral the other day and I thought about that joke, 'Nobody on their deathbed ever says they wish they had spent more time in the office.'" This elicited some hearty chuckles, but I thought, "Are you kidding me? That's exactly what every meaningful person ever said on their deathbed."

Do you honestly think Mother Teresa, on *her* deathbed, would ever have said: "Gee, I wish I hadn't spent so much time working in the orphanage. I wish I didn't take so much time caring for the sick and the dying, and raising money for my Mission of Hope"? Most spiritual leaders say the way to serve God is to serve your fellow man, and the more you serve your fellow man, the more you serve God.

You're not out there selling something someone doesn't need. When you're producing something faster, easier, higher in quality, lower in price, and your customers are paying for it, you're serving your fellow man. You need to stop thinking about when you retire, and think more about how you can better serve your customers—your fellow man!

Spirituality aside, we're all aware that the planet is in need of more goods and services to meet human needs.

Lose the idea that you're going to retire at 55. You're probably not going to retire at 60, or even 65. *And why would you want to?*

The most fun and exciting people I meet when I go out to lecture are dentists who are 70 years old and still going strong. They still love what they're doing. By now they know just about all there is to know about their patients' mouths. Sure, they may need to cut back to four days a week, then three or less, but they're still really into dentistry. The days they do work, they make a lot more money than they would on the interest of their retirement savings account.

Do you realize how hard it is to live off of interest? Do you realize (with CDs currently paying 1 percent) that for every $10,000 a year you need to live, you need $1 million in savings? If you want to retire at $50,000 a year income you would have to have $5 million in CDs paying 1 percent. Only the super rich can live off of interest today.

This old-school thought of retiring at 65, living off of Social Security and Medicare and your 401(k) for the rest of your life is *not* going to happen! Which means even more reason to reinvest in your company and focus on making it the thing you most enjoy. Life is a marathon, not a sprint. You need to be jogging at a slow, steady, enjoyable pace until you're 80 years old! I further believe that if you do, you'll actually live longer. You'll have a reason to get up every morning; you'll be doing what you love and enjoying the experience with your staff and customers.

You need to find a way to keep working and the way to do that is to keep enjoying what you do. Consider Sam Walton, the founder of Wal-Mart and Sam's Club. He found a way to sell all of the big brand names like Sony, Hitachi, and Coca-Cola with a low-cost distribution model. He had multiple myeloma at the end of his life. Instead of lying around feeling sick, he'd fly from his office in Bentonville, Arkansas, to Houston, Texas, to get his chemotherapy treatments, and then fly back to Bentonville to continue working. The man died a billionaire—and he died at his desk doing what he enjoyed. He saw his work as a mission.

Make the change before it's too late. What happens when you burn out? First thing, you'll likely want to retire. This means putting your retirement fund under tremendous pressure by attempting to live off of it too early, rather than working longer and building it up.

When people retire from work, their longevity is divided into quartiles. The men in the quartile with the lowest income at retirement live three-and-a-half years after their retirement, while those in the quartile with the highest income live six-and-a-half years on average after retirement. Why do you want to retire and start the countdown? You can blame burnout on just about anything. Besides, it's preventable. Nine times out of ten, if you're burned out, *you* are responsible.

GIVING BACK

In chapter 2, in our discussion of personal goals, I asked you to think about the person you want to be—how you wish to be remembered.

Bill Gates will forever be remembered for changing the world with Microsoft, but he stepped down from his role there and decided to put all of his efforts into the Bill & Melinda Gates Foundation, which is currently the largest operating charitable foundation in the world. Not only did he give us Microsoft, he's now putting his money to charitable use to give back to the world.

It's important for businesses to give back, not just for the sake of fiscal benefit but also for the betterment of society. A survey by Ernst & Young and the Fidelity Charitable Fund shows 89 percent (or nine out of ten) entrepreneurs donate financially—either personally or through their companies—and 70 percent donate their time. Companies that support charity are more profitable in the long run. Is it any wonder why these businesses are successful?

What can you do to give back?

Planet Earth is a seven-billion-participant marathon race. About one billion people are at the front doing five-minute miles, while about one billion more are at the back, going to bed hungry every night.

Every one at the front of this race has a moral and ethical responsibility to become more involved in community service or missionary work. Community service is giving back to your local community, while missionary work usually involves traveling far and away to some exotic corner of the earth mired in misery. You only get out of your profession and your community what you put into it. Since happiness is always an inside job, I can assure you that everyone who gets involved feels great satisfaction.

Just as colleagues share advice regarding their professions—for example, dentists share tips on performing root canals and making crowns—it is also beneficial for us to share tips and advice on giving back. What do your colleagues do as community service or for charity?

I've had several wonderful experiences with community service and mission activities within my profession.

One of my favorite dentists in the mission field is Jerome Smith of Lafayette, Louisiana. Jerome runs the Mexico Mission, which he set up with Dr. Carl Breaux and Rev. Larry Myers of Mexico Ministries in Atoyac de Alvarez, Guererro, Mexico. I had the privilege of going to Mexico with Jerome and it was unbelievable. My experience was a mix of dentistry, spirituality, a lot of camaraderie, and way too much fun. The times I've made this trip with Jerome and his crew have been among the greatest spiritual experiences of my life.

The first time I made the trip, I was carrying a lot of weight on my shoulders—dealing with the stresses of home and raising a family, along with the stress of managing a dental practice, staff, and patients. I was trying to learn endo, perio, pedo, and prostho.

I had so much on my mind, but when I arrived in Atoyac de Alvarez, and started working on people who had no electricity, sewage, or running water, all my worries melted away. It was one of the most relaxing environments I'd ever been in. The poverty these people endured was hard to imagine, yet everyone wore a smile. There were no phones or fax machines or freeways. Nobody was late for work, nobody was worrying about how much they owed on their Visa card. Nobody was stressed out—aside from the fact that they needed medical care. They were the happiest, most thankful people I'd ever encountered. I came back from that trip more energized, excited, and eager to work than if I'd gone on a two-week cruise in the Bahamas. I'm serious.

Jerome recently invited me to travel with him to Mexico, and this time I brought my sons with me. We made the trek with three dental school instructors and seven dental students from the Arizona School of Dentistry & Oral Health—A.T. Still University. It was so rewarding for me to watch these seven dental students go to work. We treated more than three hundred patients on this trip. We worked all day and then talked about dentistry until midnight every night. These students entered into the sacred and sovereign profession of dentistry for all the right reasons—treating their fellow man and doing the right thing every time. None of them is looking to "make a killing"—to work two days a week and drive Beemers and Benzes around.

My boys got to talk with these dental students and really got turned on to dentistry! I can't think of any other trip I've taken with my boys that had such a positive impact on all of us. I can retire and die in peace after witnessing the next crop of dentists getting ready to enter the profession with such passion and drive to do the right thing. They did such great work on this trip to Mexico. Dentistry is going to be in great hands. If you have any money to spare, you might consider donating to this charity. Visit www.latinworldministries.com.

Another fantastic experience was with Danny Bobrow, president of the American Dental Company and executive director of Dentists Climb for a Cause, a group that raises money by encouraging dentists to pay for fun-filled mountain climbing trips and then donates the money to the Vietnam Dental Mission. I had the pleasure to join this group to climb Mt. Adams in the state of Washington. The climb was an absolute blast, and even though there were times I thought I might freeze to death, I would do it again in a heartbeat.

Sometime in your career, you owe it to yourself to take a similar trip—for so many reasons. First, you are serving a needy population that is grateful for your help, and that is the greatest reward of going on a missionary trip.

But there are other, more subtle benefits to you. I grew up Catholic, and Catholics are big into retreats. When we were little, once a year my mom took us on these weekend retreats with the Church. We'd complain and moan about it for days, but we always returned home better for the experience. It took us out of our routines and opened our eyes to the world around us.

That's what the trip to Mexico accomplished for my sons and me.

Trips like these break your routine. You might not realize just how much time you are spending on email, texting, reading, working, and watching 24-hour news channels until you're taken out of your element. When you leave your home, leave your country, and go to a village that doesn't have an Internet connection or even a telephone, you begin to realize how weighted down you are.

I talked to my sons more during that one week in Mexico than I did the previous month. I work. They work. Our social lives rarely inter-sect. We're all preoccupied with email and texting. If we ever happen to be in the same room, at least one of us is wearing headphones, one is playing a video game, another is watching ESPN, and someone else is on the phone. We're occupying space together, but not spending as much quality time together as we should.

Another great benefit to leaving your own country is it provides the perfect opportunity to break a habit.

People develop unproductive habits, and so do businesses. Leav-ing your routine, even for a week, provides valuable time to reflect. Returning home after a week of reflection, you might realize that you're checking your email first thing in the morning when you'd be better off going for a three-mile run. A week of reflection is often the best way to break a lifetime of bad habits.

If you don't want to travel, there are ways to help that are closer to home. There are people in need within your own community. Charities I've taken part in over the years are domestic violence shelters.

Often in domestic violence situations, the man knocks out the wom-an's front tooth. The damage is cosmetically devastating and further robs the victim of her self worth. After the shelter contacts me about a woman who has suffered this injury, my team and I fix her smile for free. My mostly female staff finds this particularly touching and moti-vating. They deeply sympathize with any woman who got her tooth knocked out by a man who's supposed to love and care for her.

Here's the bottom line: I highly recommend taking yourself out of your comfort zone and serving people who really need you. *So many people need you*! Reconnect to the reason you chose your profession in the first place. If you're a plumber or a carpenter, check out Habitat for Humanity. If you own a comic book store, find out what you can do for community reading initiatives.

Service brings about a professional and spiritual awakening, I swear. Get away from your morning lattés and email. Leave your cell phone, fax machine, iMac, and iPad behind. Stop stressing about your crazy schedule, your overhead, the economy, the debt ceiling, and political debates! Ditch your life for five or ten days. Make this your vacation. Why sit on the beach like a lump for a week when you can change the lives of people who need you?

WHEN ALL IS SAID AND DONE . . .

When you retire—or, when you die—how will you be remembered by your community? Will you have made an impact?

I ask my colleagues, "Are you going to be the dentist people recall coming to this community forty years ago when the average six-year-old had three cavities, when now the average six-year-old has four?"

"Wouldn't you rather people in your community say: 'When Dr. So-and-so came to this town, kids didn't floss. Now *everyone* flosses.'"

People who trade money for time go home at night and find something to escape their dull lives: television, alcohol, drugs, food . . . These are the people who constantly complain and say they can't wait until retirement. People who work with purpose—people like Sam Walton—die at their desks.

It's time to realize your purpose! The people who live and work with a purpose don't need a 401(k). Know why? Because they're not the type of people who want to retire.

The Boy Scouts have a rule: *You always leave the campground better than you found it.* Robert Stephenson Smyth Baden-Powell, a British Army officer and the founder of scouting, wrote the original version of that rule in his last letter to the Scouts: *Try and leave this world a little better than you found it and when your turn comes to die, you can die happy in feeling that at any rate you have not wasted your time but have done your best.*

- Take time to reexamine your retirement plans.
- Ask yourself what you'd need to change about your business or career so that you'd never *want* to retire.
- Donate your time/money to organizations that need your help.

You can have everything in life you want, if you will just help other people get what they want.

—Zig Ziglar

The best way to find yourself is to lose yourself in the service of others.

—Mahatma Gandhi

At the end of life we will not be judged by how many diplomas we have received, how much money we have made, how many great things we have done. We will be judged by 'I was hungry and you gave me something to eat, I was naked and you clothed me, I was homeless and you took me in.' Hungry not only in bread—but hungry for love. Naked not only for clothing—but naked for human dignity and respect. Homeless not only for want of a room of bricks—but homeless because of rejection.

—Mother Teresa

Summary

Money is a measuring device, a way to keep track of what's going on with your business and your life. This is true for both people and time. How do you know if you are achieving your personal goals? Look at the numbers.

How do you measure whether or not the people who work with you are carrying their weight? Look at the numbers.

How do you know whether or not you are making the best use of your colleagues? Look at the numbers.

How do you know whether or not you are wasting time? Look at the numbers.

How do you measure the health of your business? Look at the numbers.

Once you have looked at the numbers, you have to look beyond them. Use your skills and resources to give back to the community. Change your attitude about retirement. Your work might change as you get older, but hopefully you will never want to retire.

Regularly examining the key numbers—net profits, cash flow, and receivables—with simple, standard financial reports is not much more difficult than flossing, and just as important.

For Further Reading

There are countless outstanding resources out there that can help you start and manage your business successfully, all of which you can integrate into your new understanding of people, time, and money. You can go through life learning everything the hard way, through trial and error, or in less than a day, you can gain the knowledge of someone who compiled a lifetime's worth of experience into a book to share with you. I am fifty years old, have an MBA and I've owned my business for twenty-five years. Yet I still read voraciously because I firmly believe that all leaders are readers. I have the personal library to prove it.

From the thousands of books I've read in the last fifty years, my favorite business author, hands down, is Jim Collins. In the first book of his that I was fortunate enough to read, *Built to Last*, Jim shares the secrets of what all the great, long-lasting companies had in common. His book *Good to Great* covers the common themes among businesses that have grown to become exceptional successes. His book *How the*

Mighty Fall focuses on the flip side—on the common reasons why businesses fail.

His most recent book, *Great by Choice,* examines the success (and failure) of great businesses in times of "uncertainty, chaos, and luck."

I consider these four to be *the* best four business books on the market today. Period. If you are thinking about quitting your day job and starting your own business, make time to devour and digest these books.

Howard's home office library, "All leaders are readers!"

Knowledge is power! I wish you the best in your business ventures. Here are some of the books that have helped me along my way, starting with the one that has meant the most to me:

- Collins, Jim, & Porras, Jerry I. (1994, 1997), *Built to Last: Successful Habits of Visionary Companies.* New York: Harper Collins Publishers.

*

- Dauten, Dale. (1999), *The Gifted Boss: How to Find, Create and Keep Great Employees.* New York: William Morrow & Company.

With respect to managing people, time and money, this is one of the best *people* books I've ever read.

*

- Blank, Arthur, and Marcus, Bernie. (2001). *Built From Scratch: How a Couple of Regular Guys Grew the Home Depot from Nothing to $30 Billion.* New York: Random House.

Learn about Home Depot's business model that conquered this country's hardware.

*

- Kroc, Ray. (1977). *Grinding It Out: The Making of McDonald's.* Chicago: Contemporary Press.

I still tell dentists to go eat at McDonald's and take a look at what the franchise behemoth will do for its customers.

*

- Vise, David A., and Malseed, Mark. (2005). *The Google Story.* New York: Random House.

Honestly, how could this fail to be a fun read?! Everyone uses Google, and the inside scoop on the company's culture is something every business should know.

*

- Grove, Andrew S. (1996). *Only the Paranoid Survive: How to Exploit the Crisis Points that Challenge Every Company.* New York: Doubleday.

Doing what you do best is bound to make you the most profit. This book is chock full of wisdom, common sense, and solid case studies from the founder of Intel. Learn what a Strategic Inflection Point is before you have to deal with one yourself.

*

- Slater, Robert. (1999). *Jack Welch & the G.E. Way: Management Insights and Leadership Secrets of the Legendary CEO.* New York: Warner Books.

Jack Welch might be one of the greatest managers of all time. Business is business whether you are making crowns, light bulbs, jet engines, or nuclear power plants.

*

- Beckwith, Harry. (1997). *Selling the Invisible: A Field Guide to Modern Marketing*. New York: Warner Books.

This book will really make you take a long, hard look at how your business markets itself just by how you operate. When you check into a hotel and find that little slip around the toilet seat, the chocolate on the pillow and the cardboard lid on the glass, *that* is selling the invisible. That tells you your room has been carefully cleaned for you without your having been there to see it. What are some ways you can sell the invisible in *your* business?

*

- Carnegie, Dale. (2009)* *How to Win Friends and Influence People*. New York: Simon & Schuster.

This timeless bestseller (©1936 by Dale Carnegie) is a must-have for anyone who owns a business. Talk about things you need to know to manage people and sell to people! Dale Carnegie wrote the bible on it and no one has topped it since.

*

- Lencioni, Patrick. (2002). *The Five Dysfunctions of a Team: A Leadership Fable*. San Francisco: Jossey-Bass.

This is another fantastic management book but it's set up in a fictional fable, which makes it just as entertaining as it is enlightening. Other books by Lencioni include: *The Advantage*; *Getting Naked*; *The Three Signs of a Miserable Job*; *Silos, Politics and Turf Wars*; *Death by Meeting*; *The Four Obsessions of an Extraordinary Executive*; *The Five Temptations of a CEO*; and *The Three Questions for a Frantic Family*. I highly recommend you read them all.

*

- Kaye, Beverly, & Jordan-Evans, Sharon. (2008). *Love 'Em or Lose 'Em: Getting Good People to Stay*. San Francisco: Berrett-Koehler Publishers.

This is the Bible of HR! If you're managing people, you must read this book!

*

- Mackay, Harvey. (2005). *Swim with the Sharks Without Being Eaten Alive: Outsell, Outmanage, Outmotivate, and Outnegotiate Your Competition*. New York: HarperCollins Publishers.

This just might be the best book on relationships on the market. I've met Harvey Mackay; he's a brilliant man. Mackay's business was selling envelopes—plain, white envelopes—and he learned how to sell more of them than anyone on the planet. How? Through customer service and relationships.

If for no other reason, buy his book for the list of *seventy-six* questions he made his sales team ask—and then record—of every customer who purchased envelopes in the United States. That way his sales team had all the information they needed to engage a customer and, ultimately, make a sale. Genius information in this book!

Index